Mental Toughness for Young Volleyball Players

Taylor Reed

Contents

Introduction   1

1. Building a Strong Foundation   5

2. Overcoming Performance Anxiety   21

3. Conquering Self-Doubt   30

4. Balancing Academics and Athletics   49

5. Enhancing Team Dynamics   59

6. Navigating Parental and Coaching Relationships   70

7. Developing Resilience and Coping Mechanisms   85

8. The Importance of Nutrition and the Mind   95

9. Drills for Success   104

10. The 7 Mental Secrets of Volleyball: Unlocking Your   113
    Peak Performance

11. Harnessing the Power of Role Models   121

Conclusion   133

A Heartfelt Thank You to Our Readers   138

We'd Love Your Feedback!   140

Introduction

It's the final set of the championship match. The score is tied 24-24, and Claire is at the service line. The entire gym is electric with tension, the crowd roaring, and the coach's voice echoing over the chaos.

"Claire, keep it steady!" Coach Smith yells.

Claire nods and sets her gaze on the opposing team's court.

"Just get it over the net," she whispers to herself, her heartbeat thundering in her ears.

As she readies her stance beyond the baseline a scary thought creeps into her mind.

What if I miss? What if I ruin everything?

Suddenly, her fear grows louder in her head with each passing second. Her hands start to tremble as she clutches the ball. The noise of the crowd turns into a distant roar, and all she can hear is her own heartbeat, pounding in her brain like a war drum. Her breath becomes shallow gasps and a feeling of panic starts clawing its way up her chest.

Claire forces herself to toss the ball into the air, her arm drawing back in what should be a fluid, practiced motion. But as the ball reaches its peak, a sudden jolt of doubt strikes her like a lightning bolt, freezing her in place. It's as if her body no longer belongs to her—her arm stiffens, her knees lock, and her heart clenches in a vice grip of fear. Time slows, the ball hanging in the air like a cruel reminder of the moment slipping away.

When her arm finally moves, it's too late. The hesitation saps her swing of both strength and precision, causing her to hit the ball awkwardly. She watches in horror as the ball flutters weakly toward the net, clips the tape and falls back to her side of the court.

Her teammates groan, the crowd exhales collectively, and Claire feels her cheeks burn.

Her mind screams at her: *Why couldn't you just focus? Why did you let them down?*

Before she can regain her composure, the ball is back in play and heading straight toward her. She tries to move into position for the dig, but her legs feel heavy, her movements sluggish and uncertain. The ball slips past her outstretched hands and crashes to the floor.

The final whistle blows, a sharp sound that cuts through her soul. The opposing team erupts in cheers, their players storming the court in a jubilant frenzy. Claire watches them celebrate, her vision blurring as tears sting her eyes. Slowly, her knees give out, and she sinks to the floor.

Claire was a skilled volleyball player, consistently excelling during practices and regular games. But when the stakes were high and the game was on the line, a familiar knot of dread would tighten in her stomach. Despite her rigorous training and efforts to stay composed, the pressure always found a way to creep in and take hold of her mind. In those decisive moments, her confidence would falter, and the anxiety she worked so hard to suppress would take over. No matter how much she tried to push through, the weight of the situation often caused her to second-guess herself, dulling her instincts and making her performance crumble under the spotlight.

If you've ever experienced a moment like Claire's—paralyzed by doubt, overwhelmed by pressure, and questioning your ability to succeed—you're not alone. In fact, even the world's top athletes, those we admire for their poise and skill, face the same internal battles. Despite their extraordinary talents, they too struggle with self-doubt, fear of failure, and the weight of expectations. The difference lies in how they handle those moments, learning to push through the mental noise and perform at their best under the same pressures we all face.

So how do the best athletes prepare for these high-stress moments? How do they stay calm, focused, and ready to perform their absolute best when the stakes couldn't be higher?

The answer? Mental Toughness.

Hello there. My name is Taylor Reed. As a former college athlete who's faced the same high-pressure moments and a sports psychologist who has spent years helping athletes overcome mental barriers, I understand the challenges you face both on and off the court. My goal with this book is to share the tools, strategies, and insights I've gained through personal experience and professional practice to help young athletes like you unlock your full potential. Together, we'll explore what it takes to build mental toughness, so you can not only succeed in your sport but thrive in life.

So how exactly do you develop mental toughness?

The good news is that mental toughness isn't something you're simply born with—it's a skill you can develop and improve. If you're ready to overcome your fears, sharpen your focus, and perform your best when it matters most, then this book is for you.

This book will serve as your guide to mastering the mental side of the game. With the right tools and strategies, you can transform pressure into power and become the player who excels in those high-stakes moments.

So, where do you start? It begins with understanding what mental toughness truly is and why it's the key to handling fear and pressure effectively. In the chapters ahead, we'll explore the psychology of performance under pressure and provide step-by-step strategies to strengthen your mental game. Chapter One is your first step—a deep dive into the fundamentals of mental toughness and how to start building a champion's mindset. Let's begin!

Chapter 1

Building a Strong Foundation

T he gym buzzed with the sounds of sneakers squeaking on polished floors and the rhythmic thud of volleyballs being spiked and served. Among the players was a young girl, smaller than the rest, her ponytail bouncing as she darted around the court. While others towered over her, she moved with precision, her eyes constantly scanning, anticipating the ball's next trajectory. She wasn't the tallest, the strongest, or the loudest, but there was something about her—an unyielding determination that set her apart.

Debbie had heard it all before. Coaches, players, even well-meaning friends told her she wasn't built for volleyball. At 5'4", she was far below the average height for a setter, let alone a player aspiring to compete at the highest levels.

"Maybe by your senior year, you'll make the varsity team," one coach had said to her father when she was in eighth grade, the words laced with doubt.

But Debbie Green Vargas wasn't one to back down from a challenge. She decided early on that she would prove them wrong, not with words, but with relentless effort. Her father's voice rang in her head during every drill, every practice: *"No one knows how good you can be, not even you. Just be better today than you were yesterday.*"

Debbie's life became a cycle of school, practice, and training. On weekdays, she spent three to four hours honing her skills, and on weekends, she practiced for nearly nine. She worked on her vertical jump, her court vision, and her agility. She knew she couldn't control her height, but she could outwork everyone else.

On one particular afternoon, the team practiced precision sets. The coach threw the ball just slightly out of reach, testing their ability to recover and deliver a perfect set. Most players struggled to reach the ball, but Debbie's quick footwork allowed her to get there in time. She felt the sting in her forearms as she delivered the set, watching the ball arc perfectly toward the hitter's hands.

"Good," the coach nodded. "Now faster."

Debbie didn't flinch. Instead, she pushed herself harder, determined to outshine her taller counterparts. She repeated the drill until her arms ached and sweat dripped down her face, but she never complained. It wasn't in her nature to quit.

Her height disadvantage became especially apparent during games. Opponents underestimated her, sending fastballs over the net to test her reflexes. Debbie loved those moments. They were chances to show that what she lacked in height, she made up for in mental sharpness and adaptability.

In one high-stakes game during her junior year, her team was trailing by three points. The opposing hitters targeted her, delivering spike after spike. The gym seemed to hold its collective breath every time the ball soared toward her. Debbie stayed calm, her focus unwavering. She crouched low, positioned her hands, and delivered precision sets despite the relentless pressure. Her sets led to three consecutive kills, tying the game and giving her team the momentum to win.

After the match, her coach approached her. "You don't play like you're 5'4"," he said. It wasn't a compliment about her height. It was recognition of her mental toughness—her ability to perform under pressure and rise above expectations.

By her junior year, Debbie's hard work earned her a spot on the USA Volleyball Team for the World Championships, making her one of the youngest players to compete on the international stage. But the pressure only mounted. Competing alongside taller, stronger teammates and opponents, she felt the weight of her perceived disadvantage more than ever.

During a particularly grueling match, Debbie faced a moment of doubt. The opposing team's blockers were relentless, towering over the net like immovable walls. Debbie hesitated for a split second, the nagging voice of doubt creeping in: *Am I good enough?*

She shook it off. *They might be taller,* she thought, *but I've prepared for this.* She focused on her fundamentals, delivering quick, unpredictable sets that threw off the blockers. Her strategic thinking and ability to stay composed under pressure turned the tide of the game, leading her team to victory.

Debbie's career culminated in the 1984 Los Angeles Olympics, where she played a pivotal role in helping the U.S. women's volleyball team secure a silver medal—the team's best finish at the time. Reflecting on her journey, she often spoke about how her mental toughness was the key to overcoming her physical limitations.

"I knew I wasn't going to get any taller," she said, "but I knew I could always improve—my vertical jump, my setting, my strategy. I could always get better."

Even after retiring from competitive play, Debbie remained a force in the volleyball world, mentoring young athletes and sharing the lessons she learned. She became a living example of how grit, perseverance, and strategic thinking could turn doubt into triumph.

Debbie Green Vargas' story reminds us all that limitations are often only as real as we let them be. She showed that the greatest victories aren't just won on the court but in the mind, where determination and mental toughness can overcome any obstacle. For every young athlete facing doubt, Debbie's journey is proof that hard work and resilience can make the impossible achievable.

Defining Mental Toughness

Mental toughness is often spoken about as the invisible force that separates good athletes from great ones. It's not about physical strength or technical prowess alone—it's about the ability to endure, adapt, and thrive under pressure. Debbie Green Vargas, one of volleyball's most celebrated setters, exemplifies this concept. Her story is a testament to how mental discipline and focus can overcome societal expectations and physical limitations.

What is Mental Toughness?

At its core, mental toughness is the ability to maintain composure, confidence, and focus in the face of adversity. It's the resilience to push through self-doubt, the discipline to outwork competitors, and the clarity to make decisions under pressure. For Debbie, mental toughness wasn't just a nice-to-have trait;

it was her lifeline in a sport where her height was seen as a disqualifier.

Focus Under Pressure

Mental toughness isn't just about training; it's about staying composed in high-stakes situations. Debbie's ability to focus under pressure became her defining trait. In one pivotal match, her team faced a stronger, taller opponent. The opposing hitters targeted Debbie, attempting to exploit her perceived weakness.

Instead of succumbing to the pressure, she used it as fuel. She analyzed their tactics, adjusted her positioning, and delivered quick, strategic sets that dismantled their game plan. Her mental clarity and adaptability turned the tide, leading her team to an unexpected victory.

These moments highlight an essential aspect of mental toughness: the ability to remain focused on what you can control, even when external circumstances seem insurmountable.

Rising Above Societal Expectations

Societal expectations often dictate what success looks like, especially in sports. Debbie's height became a constant talking point, but she refused to let it limit her. She redefined what a great setter could be, proving that success in volleyball wasn't just about physical attributes but also about mental sharpness, strategy, and heart.

Her ability to rise above these expectations wasn't accidental—it was the result of years of cultivating a mindset that valued persistence over perfection and effort over excuses. "I always felt like I had to make up for my handicap, my height," she once said. "So, I focused on everything I could control—my jump, my setting, my skills."

Lessons from Debbie's Mental Toughness

Debbie's story illustrates that mental toughness is a skill, not a trait. It's something that can be developed through deliberate practice and mindset training. Her journey offers several key lessons:

1. **Focus on What You Can Control**: Debbie couldn't change her height, but she could perfect her skills and strategy. Athletes should identify areas within their control and work relentlessly to improve them.

2. **Break Goals into Smaller Steps**: By setting incremental goals, Debbie kept herself motivated and avoided feeling overwhelmed. This approach is crucial for maintaining progress over the long term.

3. **Stay Composed Under Pressure**: Debbie's ability to focus in high-pressure situations came from her preparation. Confidence is built in practice and displayed in competition.

4. **Redefine Success on Your Terms**: Debbie didn't let societal expectations define her potential. She created her own path, proving that determination and mental sharpness could overcome physical limitations.

Characteristics of Mentally Tough Athletes

What separates good athletes from great ones isn't just skill or physical prowess—it's the mental edge. Mentally tough athletes possess a unique set of traits that enable them to rise above challenges, maintain composure under pressure, and keep pushing forward when others falter. Their resilience, focus, and ability to persevere set them apart, turning obstacles into opportunities for growth.

Let's explore the key characteristics of mentally tough athletes and how these traits can be cultivated, using examples from legendary volleyball players who embody mental toughness.

1. Resilience: Bouncing Back from Setbacks

Resilience is the ability to recover quickly from difficulties, whether it's a missed point, a tough loss, or a personal challenge. Mentally tough athletes view setbacks not as failures but as opportunities to learn and grow.

Example: Elaina Oden Elaina Oden faced constant scrutiny over her unconventional physique for volleyball. Critics questioned her ability to compete at the highest level, but she turned these doubts into motivation. Every criticism became fuel to refine her game and prove her worth. Her resilience allowed her to overcome stereotypes and become a two-time Olympian.

How to Develop Resilience:

- **Reframe setbacks**: Instead of seeing mistakes as failures, view them as lessons to improve.

- **Focus on the bigger picture**: A single loss or error doesn't define your journey.

- **Cultivate optimism**: Believe that challenges are temporary and can be overcome.

2. Focus: Maintaining Clarity Under Pressure

Mentally tough athletes have the ability to block out distractions and stay fully present in the moment. Whether they're down by several points or facing a hostile crowd, their concentration remains unshaken.

Example: Kerri Walsh Jennings During the 2004 Athens Olympics, Kerri Walsh Jennings and her partner Misty May-Treanor faced tremendous pressure. Their opponents were relentless, and the stakes couldn't have been higher. Yet Kerri's laser-sharp focus allowed her to anticipate plays, deliver precise spikes, and maintain composure. That focus was instrumental in their gold medal victory.

How to Develop Focus:

- **Practice mindfulness**: Incorporate techniques like deep breathing and visualization.

- **Set small, achievable goals**: Concentrate on one point, one play, or one task at a time.

- **Eliminate distractions**: During practice and games, learn to tune out negative thoughts and external noise.

3. Perseverance: The Commitment to Keep Going

Perseverance is about pushing through discomfort, fatigue, and adversity. Mentally tough athletes understand that success is built on consistent effort over time.

How to Cultivate Perseverance:

- **Set long-term goals**: Keep your eyes on your ultimate objective, even during tough times.

- **Embrace discomfort**: Understand that growth often comes from pushing beyond your comfort zone.

- **Find your "why"**: Stay connected to the reasons you play the sport and what motivates you.

4. Adaptability: Thriving in Change

Athletes with mental toughness are adaptable. They adjust their strategies and mindset to overcome challenges and thrive in unpredictable situations.

Example: Karch Kiraly Karch Kiraly transitioned from being a dominant indoor volleyball player to becoming one of the greatest beach volleyball players of all time. His adaptability—learning new strategies, adjusting to different conditions, and embracing a different pace of play—showcased his mental flexibility and willingness to evolve.

How to Build Adaptability:

- **Stay curious**: Approach new challenges with an open mind.

- **Be solution-oriented**: Instead of dwelling on problems, focus on finding actionable solutions.

- **Embrace change**: View change as an opportunity for

growth, not a threat.

5. Self-Belief: Confidence in One's Abilities

Confidence is the cornerstone of mental toughness. Athletes who believe in their abilities are more likely to take risks, recover from mistakes, and perform at their peak.

Example: Misty May-Treanor Misty May-Treanor often spoke about the importance of self-belief in her career. "You have to believe you're capable of anything," she once said. Her confidence allowed her to play fearlessly, leading to three Olympic gold medals alongside Kerri Walsh Jennings.

How to Build Self-Belief:

- **Celebrate small wins**: Recognize progress and accomplishments, no matter how minor.

- **Use affirmations**: Repeat positive statements about your abilities.

- **Visualize success**: Picture yourself performing at your best and achieving your goals.

6. Emotional Control: Managing Stress and Pressure

Mentally tough athletes can regulate their emotions, maintaining composure in high-pressure situations. They don't let anger, frustration, or fear derail their performance.

Example: Gabrielle Reece Gabrielle Reece was known for her calm demeanor on the court, even in the most intense moments. Her ability to manage her emotions and lead with poise inspired her teammates and helped her maintain consistency throughout her career.

How to Develop Emotional Control:

- **Practice emotional awareness**: Learn to recognize and name your emotions.

- **Use calming techniques**: Incorporate deep breathing or progressive muscle relaxation during stressful moments.

- **Reframe stress**: See pressure as an opportunity to showcase your abilities, rather than a threat.

7. Commitment to Growth: A Lifelong Learning Mindset

Mentally tough athletes are always striving to improve, whether through refining their skills, learning from mistakes, or seeking feedback. They see themselves as a work in progress.

Example: Victoria Garrick Victoria Garrick, a former USC volleyball player and mental health advocate, embodies this growth mindset. Despite facing anxiety and self-doubt during her career, she embraced her journey and used it to inspire others, proving that personal development is just as important as athletic performance.

How to Foster a Growth Mindset:

- **Learn from mistakes**: Analyze what went wrong and use it to improve.

- **Seek feedback**: Be open to constructive criticism from

coaches and teammates.

- **Stay curious**: Always look for opportunities to learn and grow, on and off the court.

Bringing It All Together

The characteristics of mentally tough athletes—resilience, focus, perseverance, adaptability, self-belief, emotional control, and a commitment to growth—are not innate qualities but skills that can be cultivated. Whether through daily practices, intentional mindset shifts, or learning from role models, these traits are within reach for any athlete willing to put in the work.

By understanding and embodying these characteristics, athletes can build the mental toughness needed to rise above challenges and reach their full potential. In the chapters ahead, we'll explore specific tools and strategies to develop these traits, inspired by the stories of volleyball legends who turned mental toughness into their greatest asset.

Common Misconceptions: The Myth of Innate Toughness

When people think of mental toughness, they often imagine it as an innate quality—a trait that some athletes are simply born with. This misconception can be discouraging for young players who may believe that they either "have it" or they don't. The truth, however, is far more empowering: mental toughness is not an inborn gift. It is a skill, just like serving, spiking, or setting, that can be learned, developed, and refined through deliberate practice and effort.

The Myth of "Natural" Mental Toughness

The idea that mental toughness is inherent stems from the way we perceive elite athletes. When we watch a player like Karch Kiraly dominate on the court or see Misty May-Treanor remain calm under Olympic pressure, it's easy to assume they've always been that way. But even the best athletes were not born mentally invincible. They struggled, doubted, and faced fears just like everyone else.

Why This Myth is Harmful

Believing that mental toughness is innate can discourage athletes in two ways:

1. **Fixed Mindset**: Players may assume that if they aren't naturally tough, they can't improve. This mindset limits growth and encourages a fear of failure.

2. **Undermining Effort**: Athletes who do show signs of mental strength may downplay the effort it took to get there, further perpetuating the myth.

The Importance of Deliberate Mental Practice

The reality is that mental toughness, like any skill, requires deliberate practice. Elite athletes don't magically develop resilience or focus—they train for it, just as they train their bodies. Here's how deliberate mental practice builds mental toughness:

1. **Consistent Training Builds Confidence** Just as physical repetition strengthens muscles, mental repetition strengthens confidence. Practicing positive self-talk, visualization, and focus exercises can create a foundation of belief that grows stronger over time. **Example**: Kerri Walsh Jennings repeatedly visualized her ideal performance before games, picturing every play in her mind. This deliberate mental preparation helped her stay calm and confident, even under the pressure of Olympic finals.

2. **Facing Challenges Strengthens Resilience** Mental toughness grows when athletes intentionally put themselves in challenging situations. Learning to manage failure and setbacks in controlled environments prepares them to handle adversity during high-stakes moments. **Example**: Misty May-Treanor's practice sessions included drills designed to simulate stressful scenarios. These drills forced her to adapt and persevere, teaching her to thrive under pressure.

3. **Reflection Promotes Growth** Athletes who deliberately analyze their mental performance—just as they review physical performance—can identify areas for improvement. Reflection transforms mistakes into opportunities and reinforces resilience. **Example**: After tough games, Gabrielle Reece often reflected on her mental state and strategies, ensuring she approached the next challenge with a clearer mindset.

How to Practice Mental Toughness

- **Set Mental Goals**: Include objectives like staying calm during high-pressure drills or maintaining focus during distractions. Treat mental skills as equal to physical skills in training.

- **Visualize Success**: Spend time imagining successful plays and positive outcomes to strengthen belief in your abilities.

- **Reframe Failure**: View setbacks as part of the learning process. Journaling after games or practices can help identify lessons and reinforce resilience.

- **Create Pressure Drills**: Simulate game-day stress during practice to build familiarity with high-pressure situations.

The Empowering Truth

The myth of innate mental toughness is just that—a myth. The most mentally tough athletes are not born; they are made through intentional practice and a commitment to growth. By embracing the mindset that mental toughness is a skill, athletes can unlock their potential and take control of their journey. Whether you're starting your volleyball career or striving for the next level, remember: mental toughness isn't something you have; it's something you build.

Reflection and Growth Worksheet

Use this worksheet to reflect on and apply the lessons from each chapter. Players and coaches can use these prompts individually or in team discussions to enhance learning and performance.

- What is mental toughness, and why is it important for volleyball?

- List three specific actions you can take daily to build mental toughness.

- Identify a mentor or role model who has helped you develop as an athlete. How have they influenced your growth?

- Reflect on a past challenge you overcame. How did mental toughness play a role?

Chapter 2

Overcoming Performance Anxiety

Allison Aldrich's journey from a small-town girl in Schuyler, Nebraska, to a Paralympic volleyball player is a testament to the power of self-belief and resilience. Born on January 19, 1988, Allison faced a life-altering challenge at the tender age of seven when she was diagnosed with sarcoma, a form of cell cancer. The aggressive nature of the disease led to the amputation of her leg, a traumatic experience that could have easily overshadowed her childhood dreams.

Despite this profound adversity, Allison's spirit remained unbroken. She found solace and strength in sports, particularly volleyball. The sport became a sanctuary where she could rebuild her confidence and redefine her identity beyond her physical limitations. Her determination to excel was evident when, in March 2004, she received an invitation to a sitting volleyball camp in Denver. This opportunity opened the door to the Paralympic arena, where she would soon make her mark.

Allison's ascent in the world of sitting volleyball was swift and remarkable. She earned her first bronze medal at the 2004 Paralympic Games in Athens, Greece. Her dedication and skill continued to shine as she secured a silver medal at the 2010 World Organization Volleyball for Disabled (WOVD) World Championships and a gold medal at the World Cup the same year. In 2011, she added two more gold medals to her collection from the ECVD Continental Cup and the Parapan American Zonal Championship (PAZC).

Throughout her journey, Allison's self-belief was a driving force. She once shared, "It has always been my philosophy that if I can do anything with my one leg, my kids can do anything with their two legs." This mindset not only propelled her athletic achievements but also inspired those around her to overcome their own challenges.

Allison's story is a powerful reminder that physical setbacks do not define one's potential. Her unwavering self-belief and determination transformed her from a young girl facing a daunting diagnosis into a celebrated athlete on the Paralympic stage. Through volleyball, she rebuilt her confidence, conquered her fears, and became a beacon of inspiration for others facing similar challenges.

Identifying Triggers of Anxiety

Anxiety often arises from uncertainty and fear of judgment, and for Allison Aldrich, these emotions were particularly intense as she navigated life and competitive sports with a prosthesis. Her journey to becoming a Paralympic medalist wasn't just about physical rehabilitation—it was also about confronting and managing the mental hurdles that came with her new reality.

Facing Anxiety in a New Reality

When Allison began playing volleyball with a prosthetic leg, she couldn't help but feel a heightened awareness of her difference. The worry wasn't just about whether she could keep up physically, but also how others—teammates, opponents, and even spectators—might perceive her.

"The hardest part wasn't learning how to play with a prosthesis," she once reflected. "It was convincing myself that I belonged on the court." This inner dialogue, filled with self-doubt and uncertainty, became one of Allison's greatest challenges.

Her anxiety often surfaced in specific moments:

- **Entering new environments**: Joining teams or walking into tournaments, she feared being labeled as "different."

- **High-pressure plays**: During pivotal moments in games, the thought of failing or letting her team down magnified her nervousness.

- **Facing visible judgment**: The stares or whispers of onlookers served as constant reminders of her amputation, triggering self-consciousness.

Recognizing Anxiety Triggers

Allison's first step toward managing her anxiety was learning to identify its triggers. She became more attuned to the physical and emotional signs—racing thoughts, a tight chest, or a sudden feeling of dread. By journaling her experiences, she discovered patterns in when and where her anxiety was most likely to emerge.

- **Reflection after games**: Allison wrote about moments that made her uneasy, analyzing whether they were caused by external pressures or her own fears.

- **Seeking feedback**: She spoke openly with her coaches and teammates, asking for their observations on her performance and demeanor. Their reassurances helped her recognize when her anxiety was unfounded.

Managing Triggers Through Mindset and Routine

Once Allison identified her triggers, she developed strategies to manage them:

1. **Mental Reframing**: Instead of focusing on what she couldn't control—like how others viewed her—she redirected her energy toward what she could control: her skills and mindset. "I realized that I wasn't just representing myself but also others with disabilities. That thought empowered me."

2. **Grounding Techniques**: Before games, Allison practiced deep breathing exercises to center herself. This simple routine helped her calm her racing thoughts and stay present in the moment.

3. **Positive Visualization**: She spent time imagining herself succeeding—delivering perfect sets, diving for

saves, and celebrating victories. By focusing on these positive outcomes, she replaced fear with confidence.

4. **Open Communication**: By sharing her anxieties with trusted mentors, teammates, and coaches, Allison found a support system that reminded her she was not alone.

Transforming Anxiety into Strength

Over time, Allison's anxiety triggers became less daunting as she mastered her response to them. She used the nervous energy that once paralyzed her to fuel her competitive drive. When entering new environments or high-stakes games, she reminded herself of her journey—the obstacles she had already overcome—and used that as a foundation for confidence.

Allison's ability to face and manage her anxiety not only elevated her performance on the court but also made her a role model for others. By understanding her triggers and developing strategies to address them, she turned her vulnerabilities into strengths, proving that true mental toughness begins with self-awareness.

Mindfulness Techniques for Young Athletes

Mindfulness is the practice of staying present and aware in the moment, and for athletes like Allison Aldrich, it became an invaluable tool in managing stress and anxiety during competitions. By using techniques such as breathing exercises and visualization, Allison transformed moments of doubt into opportunities for focus and clarity.

The Power of Breath Control

Allison discovered early in her volleyball career that controlling her breath was a simple yet powerful way to calm her nerves. Before each game, as the weight of expectation began to creep in, she would find a quiet moment to center herself.

One of her go-to methods was **box breathing**—a technique that involves inhaling for four counts, holding the breath for four counts, exhaling for four counts, and then pausing for another four counts. "It felt like hitting a reset button," Allison explained. "When my thoughts spiraled, focusing on my breath brought me back to the present."

During critical moments in games, such as a tie-breaking serve or a game-deciding rally, Allison leaned on this technique to maintain her composure. Her steady breath helped her channel her focus, ensuring that she could execute her role with precision.

Visualization for Confidence and Preparation

Visualization was another key component of Allison's mindfulness practice. Before games, she would close her eyes and picture herself on the court, moving confidently and executing plays flawlessly. She imagined the feel of the ball in her hands, the sound of her teammates' encouragement, and the energy of a well-timed spike.

"I didn't just see success," she said. "I felt it. I rehearsed it in my mind so many times that when I stepped onto the court, it was like I had already been there."

Visualization not only prepared Allison for physical execution but also replaced her self-doubt with a sense of readiness. This practice became a cornerstone of her mental routine, one that any young athlete can adopt to build confidence and focus.

Transforming Nervous Energy into Focused Power

Nerves are an inevitable part of competition, but Allison Aldrich learned to see them not as a weakness but as a source of strength. Her journey to mastering nervous energy is a powerful example of how athletes can turn anxiety into a tool for peak performance.

The Shift from Fear to Excitement

Early in her career, Allison's nerves often felt overwhelming, especially during pivotal moments in games. Over time, she re-framed her perspective on nervous energy. Instead of interpreting her racing heart and heightened senses as fear, she began to see them as signs that her body was preparing for action.

"Nervous energy is just excitement in disguise," she often reminded herself. By making this mental shift, Allison was able to harness her adrenaline to sharpen her focus rather than cloud her judgment.

Channeling Energy Into Performance

One of Allison's most memorable performances came during the 2008 Paralympic Games. The match was tied, and her team needed a flawless set to secure the point. The pressure was immense, and Allison could feel her nerves building as the opposing team prepared to serve.

Instead of succumbing to the tension, she used the surge of energy to lock in on her role. She focused on her breathing, grounded herself, and reminded herself of her preparation. The ball came her way, and with precise hands and a clear mind, she delivered a perfect set that led to the game-winning spike.

"That moment wasn't about the absence of nerves," Allison later reflected. "It was about embracing them and letting them fuel my focus."

Practical Strategies for Athletes

Allison's ability to turn nervous energy into focused power offers valuable lessons for young athletes:

- **Ground Yourself**: Use physical anchors, like focusing on the feel of the ball or the sound of the court, to stay present.

- **Reframe Nervousness**: Remind yourself that nerves are a sign of readiness, not weakness.

- **Set Small, Immediate Goals**: Instead of thinking about the entire game, focus on one point, one play, or one action at a time.

By embracing these strategies, Allison turned what once felt like a hurdle into one of her greatest strengths. Her story reminds us that nervous energy, when channeled effectively, can be the spark that ignites extraordinary performance.

Reflection and Growth Worksheet

Use this worksheet to reflect on and apply the lessons from each chapter. Players and coaches can use these prompts individually or in team discussions to enhance learning and performance.

- What are your biggest triggers for anxiety during volleyball games?

- Write down two mindfulness or breathing techniques you can use during high-pressure moments.

- Recall a time when anxiety affected your performance. What steps could you take next time to manage it better?

- Create a personal "trigger response plan" to stay calm and focused during tough situations.

Chapter 3

Conquering Self-Doubt

Elaina Oden's journey to becoming a two-time Olympian is not just a story of athletic excellence—it's a testament to overcoming self-doubt and learning to embrace one's own uniqueness. Born into a volleyball-loving family in Orange, California, Elaina grew up surrounded by the sport. Her sisters, Kim and Beverly, were standout athletes in their own right, and the family's dedication to volleyball set a high bar. Yet for Elaina, the road to greatness was deeply intertwined with a struggle to accept her body and recognize her own potential.

The Struggles of Self-Image

Elaina didn't fit the mold of the typical volleyball player. As a tall, strong young woman with a powerful build, she often felt out of place in a sport that celebrated lean, agile physiques. Her broad shoulders and muscular frame set her apart, and she internalized those differences as flaws.

"I always felt like my body wasn't what people expected," she later admitted. "I was strong, but in a way that didn't fit the typical image of a volleyball player. That stuck with me for a long time." These insecurities followed her onto the court, making her question her abilities and whether she truly belonged among her peers.

Early Triumphs and Lingering Doubt

Despite her reservations, Elaina's natural talent was undeniable. At Irvine High School, she excelled in volleyball, basketball, soccer, softball, and track and field, becoming the state champion in the shot put during her senior year. Yet even with these accolades, her doubts persisted. Her strength, which was an asset in competition, felt like a liability when it came to fitting societal expectations.

When Elaina joined the University of the Pacific's volleyball team, she was thrust into an environment that demanded both physical and mental toughness. Her coach, John Dunning, recognized her potential and pushed her to embrace her strengths rather than shy away from them. "Elaina had something special," Dunning recalled. "But she needed to see it in herself."

Steps to Overcome Self-Doubt

Elaina didn't transform overnight. Her journey to self-acceptance and elite performance was the result of deliberate steps and a shift in mindset:

1. **Leaning into Her Strengths:** Instead of trying to fit into the traditional mold, Elaina began to focus on what made her unique. Her strength and power became her greatest assets as a middle blocker, allowing her to dominate at the net. "I realized that my body wasn't a weakness—it was my greatest tool," she said. This shift in

perspective helped her embrace her build and play to her strengths.

2. **Developing Mental Resilience:** Elaina worked closely with her coaches to develop mental toughness. She practiced visualization, picturing herself using her power to outmaneuver opponents. She also adopted a mantra: *"I'm here for a reason, and I have something to prove."* This mental preparation helped her silence self-doubt and focus on her game.

3. **Setting Incremental Goals:** Elaina broke her progress into smaller, achievable milestones. Whether it was perfecting a particular move or improving her vertical jump, these victories built her confidence and proved to her that she was capable of excelling at the highest level.

4. **Building a Support Network:** Her teammates and family played a crucial role in her transformation. Her sisters, who faced challenges of their own, encouraged her to keep pushing forward. Her coaches provided constructive feedback, helping her see how her unique attributes could be harnessed to dominate on the court.

Rising to the Top

By her junior year, Elaina was unstoppable. She led the University of the Pacific to back-to-back NCAA national championships in 1985 and 1986, earning All-American honors as a middle blocker. Her ability to harness her power, combined with her growing mental resilience, made her one of the most formidable players in college volleyball.

Despite a knee injury that sidelined her for the 1988 Olympics, Elaina's perseverance brought her back stronger than ever. She represented the U.S. Women's National Volleyball Team at the 1992 Olympics in Barcelona, helping secure a bronze medal. She went on to compete again in the 1996 Atlanta Games, cementing her legacy as one of the sport's greats.

Lessons in Confidence and Self-Acceptance

Reflecting on her journey, Elaina often spoke about the importance of embracing what makes you different. "I stopped trying to be what I thought people wanted and started focusing on being the best version of myself," she said. This lesson extended beyond the court, inspiring young athletes to see their differences as strengths rather than obstacles.

Elaina Oden's story is a powerful reminder that greatness doesn't come from fitting into a mold—it comes from breaking it. By learning to embrace her unique physique and channel her power into her game, she not only overcame her self-doubt but also became a role model for athletes everywhere. For anyone facing insecurity or fear of judgment, her journey offers a blueprint for turning perceived weaknesses into undeniable strengths.

Rewriting Negative Thoughts: A Mental Gamechanger for Athletes

Athletes are often celebrated for their physical prowess, but their mental game is just as crucial—if not more so—in determining success. Yet, even the most elite athletes can fall prey to negative thoughts. The good news? With the right techniques, these thoughts can be rephrased into positive affirmations that empower rather than hinder.

The Challenge of Negative Thinking in Sports

Whether it's reliving a missed play or worrying about future performance, athletes can become stuck in a cycle of negative thinking. This mindset not only affects their mental health but can also impact their physical performance. Negative thoughts often lead to increased stress, decreased focus, and self-doubt—all of which can derail an athlete's game.

The Impact of Reframing Thoughts

The key to breaking free from this cycle lies in reframing those negative thoughts. Reframing doesn't mean ignoring reality or pretending mistakes didn't happen. Instead, it's about acknowledging the situation and choosing to focus on a constructive perspective.

For example:

- Instead of "I always mess up under pressure," reframe it to: "I've worked hard to prepare for this, and I'm ready to handle the pressure."

- Instead of "I'll never be as good as my teammates," think: "I bring unique strengths to my team, and I can continue to improve."

These shifts in perspective can reduce stress and increase confidence, creating a foundation for better performance.

Practical Strategies for Rephrasing Negative Thoughts

Athletes can use the following steps to turn negativity into motivation:

1. **Identify the Negative Thought**: Start by recognizing when you're stuck in a negative mindset. Write down the thought as it comes to mind.

2. **Challenge Its Validity**: Ask yourself if the thought is entirely true. Often, negative thoughts are exaggerated or based on emotions rather than facts.

3. **Reframe the Thought Positively**: Replace the negative statement with one that is optimistic, affirming, and motivating. Ensure it's realistic and focused on personal growth.

4. **Practice Affirmations Regularly**: Reinforce positive thinking by repeating affirmations, such as "I am capable of handling challenges" or "I've improved with every practice."

5. **Visualize Success**: Pair your reframed thoughts with mental imagery of positive outcomes, such as executing a perfect play or succeeding under pressure.

The Role of Coaches and Support Systems

Coaches, teammates, and family members play a vital role in

helping athletes manage their mental health. Offering constructive feedback, modeling positive reinforcement, and fostering
an environment that values effort over perfection can all help
athletes shift their focus away from self-criticism.

Long-Term Benefits of Positive Reframing

Reframing negative thoughts isn't just about improving performance—it also builds resilience, reduces anxiety, and boosts
overall mental well-being. For athletes, these benefits translate
into a more focused, confident, and balanced approach to both
sports and life.

Conclusion

Negative thinking doesn't have to control an athlete's performance. By learning to recognize, challenge, and reframe these
thoughts, athletes can regain control of their mindset, turning
their mental game into one of their greatest strengths. Just
as physical skills are honed with practice, so too can mental
resilience be developed with deliberate effort, paving the way
for sustained success on and off the field.

Celebrating Small Wins: Building Confidence and Joy in Youth Athletes

In the fast-paced world of youth sports, the focus often leans
heavily on winning games and achieving milestones. But there's
another approach—one that fosters long-term growth, confidence, and happiness: celebrating small wins. These incremental victories, whether big or small, play a critical role in shaping
young athletes into resilient and motivated players.

Why Small Wins Matter

Small wins are more than just stepping stones to bigger goals—they are powerful confidence boosters that encourage young athletes to embrace challenges with a positive mindset. Each time a player masters a new skill, overcomes a fear, or achieves a minor goal, they are reminded of their progress and potential.

By shifting the focus from results to growth, parents and coaches can create an environment where youth athletes feel valued and supported, regardless of the outcome of the game. This approach helps reduce pressure, minimize burnout, and nurture a genuine love for the sport.

The Psychological Power of Small Wins

Small wins have a cumulative psychological effect. Celebrating them provides immediate positive reinforcement, motivating athletes to keep pushing forward. When athletes recognize their progress, they begin to associate effort with success, reinforcing a growth mindset.

For example:

- A young soccer player might struggle with penalty kicks during practice. After hitting the target once, they receive positive feedback from their coach, fueling their desire to try again.

- A swimmer shaving off just a fraction of a second from their personal best is a cause for celebration, reminding them that every effort counts.

Recognizing these moments keeps athletes focused on improvement rather than perfection, reducing anxiety and building resilience.

How to Celebrate Small Wins

Parents and coaches play a pivotal role in highlighting and celebrating small wins. Here are some practical ways to make those moments count:

1. **Acknowledge Effort and Growth** Praise athletes for their hard work and dedication, even if the results aren't perfect. For instance, if a volleyball player successfully attempts a new serve for the first time, acknowledge their courage and improvement.

2. **Create a Positive Environment** Foster a team culture that values progress over perfection. Celebrate individual and collective achievements, such as improved communication during a match or a teammate's first successful dig.

3. **Set Incremental Goals** Help athletes set realistic and achievable milestones. Whether it's mastering a new skill or showing improved focus during practice, these goals provide clear markers for progress.

4. **Use Specific Praise** Replace generic comments like "Good job!" with specific feedback, such as "I loved how you kept your eye on the ball during that play." This re-

inforces the behavior you want to see and helps athletes understand what they're doing well.

5. **Incorporate Fun Rewards** Celebrating doesn't always have to be elaborate. Simple gestures like high-fives, stickers, or a shoutout during team meetings can make a big impact. For team-wide achievements, consider fun activities like a group pizza party or a day of relaxed drills.

Building Long-Term Confidence and Joy

Celebrating small wins not only boosts confidence in the short term but also nurtures a love for the sport that lasts. When athletes feel supported and valued for their progress, they are more likely to stick with their sport, overcome setbacks, and embrace challenges with determination.

Parents and coaches who focus on small wins help create a culture where athletes learn to appreciate the journey, not just the destination. By shifting the narrative from "Did we win?" to "What did we achieve today?" youth athletes can experience the joy and growth that comes from their efforts.

Conclusion

In the competitive landscape of youth sports, it's easy to lose sight of the little things. But by celebrating small wins, we can empower young athletes to build confidence, foster resilience, and find true joy in their sport. These moments, though small, have the power to leave a lasting impact—both on and off the field.

The Courage to Acknowledge Mistakes Without Self-Judgment

Mistakes are an inevitable part of life. From small slip-ups to larger missteps, they remind us of our humanity. Yet, for many, acknowledging mistakes without spiraling into self-judgment can be a daunting challenge. Instead of seeing errors as opportunities for growth, we often view them as personal failures, allowing feelings of shame and inadequacy to take over. But what if we shifted our perspective? What if mistakes could be stepping stones toward self-improvement and resilience?

Mistakes as a Natural Part of Growth

Making mistakes isn't just common—it's necessary for learning and development. Whether you're learning a new skill, navigating relationships, or managing responsibilities, errors provide valuable feedback. They highlight what doesn't work, paving the way for more informed decisions and better strategies moving forward.

The Trap of Self-Judgment

When mistakes occur, many of us fall into the trap of self-judgment. Instead of addressing the situation objectively, we let harsh inner dialogue take over: *"I'm such a failure,"* or *"Why can't I get it right?"* This kind of thinking doesn't just lower self-esteem—it stifles our ability to learn and move forward.

Self-judgment often stems from perfectionism or the unrealistic expectation that we must always have the "right" answers. When we fall short, it feels like a personal flaw rather than a normal part of the human experience. Breaking free from this mindset requires a conscious effort to separate our actions from our identity.

Shifting Toward Self-Compassion

Self-compassion is the antidote to self-judgment. Instead of berating ourselves for our mistakes, self-compassion invites us to approach them with kindness and understanding. This doesn't mean excusing or ignoring errors—it means treating ourselves with the same patience and care we'd offer a friend.

Here's how to cultivate self-compassion:

1. **Acknowledge the Mistake**: Accept that it happened without assigning blame or guilt. For example, "I missed the deadline, and that's okay. I'll do better next time."

2. **Practice Self-Kindness**: Replace negative self-talk with affirmations. Instead of saying, "I'm terrible at this," say, "I'm learning, and that's a process."

3. **Embrace Your Humanity**: Remind yourself that mistakes are universal. Everyone falters, and you're no exception.

The Role of Reflection

Acknowledging mistakes without self-judgment requires thoughtful reflection. Reflection isn't about dwelling on what went wrong—it's about understanding why it happened and how to improve. Consider these steps:

- **Analyze the Root Cause**: Was the mistake due to a lack of preparation, a misunderstanding, or something beyond your control? Identifying the cause helps you prevent it from recurring.

- **Extract the Lesson**: What did this mistake teach you? Perhaps it revealed a gap in knowledge or the need for clearer communication.

- **Set New Intentions**: Use your insights to create actionable steps for the future. For example, if poor time management led to your mistake, commit to better planning.

The Courage to Move Forward

Acknowledging mistakes takes courage, especially when the instinct is to bury them or blame others. It requires humility to admit missteps and a willingness to grow from them. But each time you approach a mistake with compassion and curiosity, you strengthen your resilience.

As the article notes, "By owning our imperfections, we become more authentic." Authenticity isn't about being flawless—it's about being real. And real people make mistakes, learn from them, and continue striving toward their goals.

Conclusion: Redefining Mistakes

Mistakes don't define us. What defines us is how we respond to them. By letting go of self-judgment and embracing mistakes as opportunities, we can transform setbacks into powerful moments of growth. It takes courage, yes, but it's a courage that leads to deeper self-awareness, greater compassion, and a life lived with authenticity and purpose.

Breaking Free from Perfectionism in Athletes

Perfectionism is often celebrated as a driving force behind achievement, especially in sports. After all, striving for excellence and pushing boundaries is what helps athletes reach the top, right? But perfectionism isn't always the asset it appears to be. For many athletes, the relentless pursuit of flawlessness comes with a hidden cost: increased stress, fear of failure, and a paralyzing inability to take risks.

Understanding and managing perfectionism is crucial for athletes who want to perform their best without sacrificing their mental well-being.

What is Perfectionism in Athletes?

Perfectionism is the constant pressure to meet impossibly high standards, often coupled with an intense fear of making mistakes. While it can motivate athletes to work hard, it frequently becomes counterproductive when they feel their worth hinges solely on their performance.

Perfectionism typically manifests in two forms:

1. **Adaptive Perfectionism**: This involves high standards paired with a balanced perspective. Athletes with adaptive perfectionism strive for excellence but can accept

setbacks as part of the process.

2. **Maladaptive Perfectionism**: This form is more harmful, characterized by extreme self-criticism, fear of failure, and an all-or-nothing mindset.

For athletes with maladaptive perfectionism, even minor mistakes can feel like monumental failures, leading to a cycle of stress, doubt, and burnout.

The Impact of Perfectionism on Athletes

While the drive for improvement is essential in sports, unchecked perfectionism can have detrimental effects, including:

- **Increased Anxiety**: Constantly striving for flawlessness leaves little room for error, making athletes overly anxious about performing.

- **Fear of Failure**: Athletes may become so afraid of failing that they avoid taking risks altogether, hindering growth and adaptability.

- **Low Self-Esteem**: Perfectionism often ties self-worth directly to success, leaving athletes feeling inadequate if they fall short.

- **Burnout**: The relentless pursuit of perfection can lead to physical and mental exhaustion, reducing an athlete's ability to enjoy their sport.

For instance, an athlete who focuses solely on winning every match might overlook their progress or fail to appreciate the joy of the game. Over time, this can drain their passion and motivation.

How to Manage Perfectionism in Sports

Recognizing and addressing perfectionism is essential for athletes to thrive. Here are strategies to help break free from its grip:

1. Reframe Mistakes as Learning Opportunities

Instead of viewing mistakes as failures, see them as part of the process. Mistakes are valuable teaching moments that highlight areas for growth and improvement. Legendary athletes like Serena Williams often credit their setbacks for shaping their resilience and drive.

2. Set Realistic Goals

Replace all-or-nothing goals with achievable, incremental ones. For example, rather than aiming for a perfect season, focus on mastering a specific skill or improving one aspect of performance. Realistic goals help athletes feel a sense of accomplishment without unnecessary pressure.

3. Practice Self-Compassion

Athletes should treat themselves with the same kindness they'd offer a teammate. When things don't go as planned, practice self-talk like, "It's okay to make mistakes. This is part of my journey."

4. Celebrate Effort, Not Just Results

Shift the focus from outcomes to effort. Coaches and parents play a crucial role here by recognizing hard work and dedication, even when the scoreboard doesn't reflect success.

5. Create a Balanced Perspective

Understand that no one can be perfect all the time. A missed shot or a poor performance doesn't erase an athlete's skills or value. By zooming out to see the bigger picture, athletes can better appreciate their progress.

6. Embrace Risks and Experimentation

Encourage athletes to try new strategies or techniques, even if it means failing at first. Taking risks fosters growth and builds resilience.

7. Work with Mental Health Professionals

Sports psychologists and counselors can help athletes develop healthier mindsets, offering tools to manage perfectionism and reduce performance anxiety.

Turning Perfectionism into a Strength

Perfectionism doesn't have to be a barrier. When managed effectively, it can fuel an athlete's desire to improve while maintaining balance. Adaptive perfectionism—striving for excellence without the fear of failure—can help athletes stay motivated, focused, and resilient.

By embracing imperfection, athletes free themselves to take risks, learn, and ultimately perform at their best. As Olympic swimmer Michael Phelps once said, "It's not how you start; it's how you finish."

Conclusion: Redefining Success

For athletes, success isn't about being flawless—it's about progress, perseverance, and passion. By recognizing the pitfalls of perfectionism and adopting strategies to manage it, athletes can find freedom in their sport, perform with confidence, and enjoy the journey as much as the destination.

Reflection and Growth Worksheet

Use this worksheet to reflect on and apply the lessons from each chapter. Players and coaches can use these prompts individually or in team discussions to enhance learning and performance.

- What negative thoughts do you often experience before or during games?

- Reframe one of these thoughts into a positive, empowering statement.

- Identify three "small wins" you've achieved recently in

volleyball. How did they build your confidence?

- Reflect on a mistake you made. What lesson did you learn, and how will you use it to improve?

Chapter 4

Balancing Academics and Athletics

K erri Walsh Jennings, a three-time Olympic gold medalist in beach volleyball, is celebrated for her exceptional athletic achievements. However, her journey to the pinnacle of her sport was marked by significant challenges, including self-doubt and the demanding task of balancing academics and athletics during her collegiate years at Stanford University.

From a young age, Kerri exhibited remarkable athletic talent. Growing up in Santa Clara, California, she was deeply passionate about volleyball. However, like many young athletes, she grappled with self-doubt. Reflecting on her career, Kerri once shared, "I think a lot of people think that the injuries and the losses have been the hardest part of my career, but the No.1 thing (actually) has been my self-doubt."

In 1996, Kerri enrolled at Stanford University, a prestigious institution known for its rigorous academics and competitive athletics. As a student-athlete, she faced the formidable challenge of excelling both in the classroom and on the volleyball court. This required meticulous time management and unwavering dedication. Kerri's commitment to her sport was evident;

she mentioned, "Generally, I'll have three training sessions a day."

Balancing such an intense training schedule with academic responsibilities demanded exceptional discipline. Kerri's approach involved setting clear priorities and maintaining a structured routine. She emphasized the importance of surrounding oneself with a supportive network, stating, "You have to rely on your support system. Growing up, I always thought it was a sign of weakness to ask for help, but now I realize it's really a sign of strength to say, 'I need help, I can't do it all.'"

Her time at Stanford was not only about honing her athletic skills but also about personal growth and overcoming self-doubt. Kerri's resilience and determination were instrumental in her development. She believed that "Adversity, if you allow it to, will fortify you and make you the best you can be."

Kerri's collegiate years laid a solid foundation for her illustrious career in beach volleyball. Her ability to balance the demands of academics and athletics, coupled with her determination to overcome self-doubt, serves as an inspiring example for aspiring athletes. Her journey underscores the significance of perseverance, effective time management, and the courage to seek support when needed.

Time Management Strategies for Student-Athletes: Lessons from Kerri Walsh Jennings

Balancing academics and athletics is a challenging endeavor, one that requires discipline, structure, and a clear sense of priorities. During her time at Stanford University, Kerri Walsh Jennings exemplified how meticulous planning and dedication could help a student-athlete thrive in both arenas.

Structuring the Day: The Power of Routine

For Kerri, time management started with creating a structured daily routine. She broke her day into manageable blocks, dedicating specific times to academics, training, recovery, and personal downtime. This method allowed her to focus on one task at a time, minimizing distractions and stress.

A typical day for Kerri might have looked like this:

- **Morning:** Academic classes and study sessions. Kerri believed in starting her day with focus, ensuring her coursework received the attention it deserved before practice demands took over.

- **Afternoon:** Volleyball practice and strength training. She scheduled her athletic commitments during peak energy hours, ensuring she could perform at her best.

- **Evening:** Homework, group study sessions, or reviewing class material. Kerri used this time to reinforce what she had learned earlier in the day.

- **Night:** Rest and recovery. Kerri prioritized sleep, understanding its vital role in both academic retention and athletic recovery.

This structured approach helped her avoid the common pitfall of procrastination, ensuring she stayed ahead in both her studies and her sport.

Prioritizing Commitments

Kerri was also skilled at prioritizing her commitments. She understood that not every task could be tackled simultaneously, so she ranked her responsibilities based on urgency and importance. This allowed her to focus on high-priority tasks without feeling overwhelmed.

For example:

- During the volleyball season, Kerri might adjust her study schedule to account for travel and competitions, completing assignments ahead of time.

- When preparing for exams, she scaled back on extra-curricular activities to devote more hours to academic preparation.

Her ability to adapt her priorities ensured she maintained balance without sacrificing excellence in either domain.

The Role of Planning Tools

Kerri relied on planning tools to stay organized. Whether it was a detailed planner, a calendar app, or simply jotting down her tasks for the day, she ensured every hour was accounted for. By visually mapping out her schedule, she could anticipate busy weeks and plan accordingly.

Her method aligns with modern time-blocking strategies, where each task is allocated a specific period. This approach maximizes productivity by creating a clear framework for the day.

Staying Flexible Under Pressure

While structure was key, Kerri also recognized the need for flexibility. Unexpected changes—like an extended practice or a last-minute group project—required her to adjust her plans. Rather than viewing these disruptions as setbacks, she embraced them as opportunities to practice adaptability.

"If something didn't go as planned, I'd remind myself to stay focused on what I could control," Kerri shared in an interview. Her ability to stay calm and pivot her schedule kept her on track, even during challenging times.

The Takeaway for Student-Athletes

Kerri's success as a student-athlete at Stanford serves as a model for balancing demanding commitments. Her approach offers valuable lessons for young athletes:

- **Plan Your Day:** Create a routine that prioritizes academics, training, and recovery.

- **Rank Your Tasks:** Focus on what's most important to avoid feeling overwhelmed.

- **Use Tools to Stay Organized:** Planners, calendars, and reminders can keep you on track.

- **Stay Flexible:** Be prepared to adjust your schedule when unexpected challenges arise.

- **Prioritize Rest:** Remember that adequate sleep is non-negotiable for peak performance.

By following these strategies, student-athletes can take control of their schedules and set themselves up for success both on and off the court, just as Kerri did.

Stress Management for Busy Athletes

Being a student-athlete is no easy feat. Balancing rigorous academic responsibilities with demanding athletic schedules often leads to significant stress. Without proper management, this stress can impact performance, health, and overall well-being. Learning to manage stress effectively is critical for athletes who want to perform their best while maintaining a healthy mindset.

Understanding the Sources of Stress

For athletes, stress often stems from multiple areas:

- **Time Constraints:** Juggling classes, practice, games, and social commitments can leave little room to breathe.

- **Performance Pressure:** The desire to excel in both sports and academics can lead to self-imposed expectations and fear of failure.

- **Fatigue:** Long hours of training and study can lead to physical and mental exhaustion.

- **Unrealistic Expectations:** Athletes may feel pressure from coaches, peers, and even themselves to meet high standards.

Recognizing these stressors is the first step in managing them effectively.

Practical Stress-Management Techniques

1. Prioritize and Plan

Creating a clear plan for the day or week can reduce the feeling of being overwhelmed. Using tools like planners or scheduling apps helps athletes visualize their responsibilities and allocate time for each task. By staying organized, athletes can reduce last-minute scrambling and the stress it brings.

2. Incorporate Mindfulness Practices

Mindfulness techniques, such as meditation and deep breathing, are powerful tools for calming the mind. Athletes can spend just a few minutes each day practicing mindfulness to reduce stress and increase focus.

- **Breathing Exercises:** Techniques like box breathing (inhaling for 4 counts, holding for 4, exhaling for 4, and holding for 4) can provide instant relaxation during high-stress moments.

- **Guided Meditation:** Apps like Headspace or Calm offer quick meditations tailored for stress relief, ideal for busy athletes.

3. Break Tasks Into Smaller Steps

Large assignments or long-term goals can feel daunting. Breaking them into smaller, manageable tasks can make them less intimidating. Completing each step provides a sense of accomplishment, helping reduce overall stress.

4. Prioritize Sleep

Sleep is essential for recovery and stress management. A lack of sleep exacerbates anxiety, reduces focus, and weakens physical performance. Athletes should aim for 7–9 hours of quality sleep each night and establish a pre-sleep routine to wind down after busy days.

Managing Stress During Competition

Athletes often face heightened stress during games or events. Here are strategies to stay calm and focused under pressure:

- **Visualize Success:** Mentally rehearsing plays or movements can instill confidence and reduce anxiety.

- **Stay in the Moment:** Focus on the immediate task rather than worrying about the outcome. For example, think about the next serve rather than the final score.

- **Lean on Your Team:** Teammates can be a great source of encouragement during stressful moments. Relying on one another fosters trust and reduces feelings of isolation.

Building a Support System

No athlete should navigate stress alone. Coaches, teammates, family, and friends can offer valuable support. Open communication about stressors allows others to provide encouragement or assistance. Seeking help from sports psychologists or counselors can also be beneficial, offering tailored techniques to handle stress effectively.

Recognizing When Stress Becomes Overwhelming

While some stress is normal, excessive or chronic stress can be harmful. Signs of overwhelming stress include:

- Persistent fatigue

- Irritability or mood swings

- Trouble concentrating

- Physical symptoms like headaches or muscle tension

If these symptoms persist, athletes should seek professional help to develop personalized coping strategies.

Conclusion: Thriving Under Pressure

Stress is an inevitable part of being a busy athlete, but it doesn't have to be debilitating. With proactive planning, mindfulness practices, and a strong support system, athletes can manage stress effectively and thrive in their dual roles. As Kerri Walsh Jennings once said, "Pressure is a privilege—it's a reminder that you're in a position to do something great." By learning to manage stress, athletes can turn challenges into opportunities and reach their full potential.

Reflection and Growth Worksheet

Use this worksheet to reflect on and apply the lessons from each chapter. Players and coaches can use these prompts individually or in team discussions to enhance learning and performance.

- How do you currently manage your time between school and volleyball?

- Create a sample daily schedule that includes time for practice, study, and relaxation.

- List three strategies to handle stress during busy weeks.

- Reflect on a moment when you successfully balanced both academics and sports. What did you do well?

Chapter 5
Enhancing Team Dynamics

M isty May-Treanor and Kerri Walsh Jennings are celebrated as one of the most formidable duos in beach volleyball history, clinching three consecutive Olympic gold medals in 2004, 2008, and 2012. Their unparalleled success was deeply rooted in mutual trust, seamless communication, and profound respect for each other.

Born on July 30, 1977, in Los Angeles, California, Misty May-Treanor was introduced to volleyball at an early age. Her father, Butch May, was a 1968 Olympian in volleyball, and her mother, Barbara, was a nationally ranked tennis player. Despite her athletic lineage, Misty faced personal challenges, including navigating an abusive childhood. However, she remained determined to carve her own path in the sport she loved. Reflecting on her motivation, Misty shared, "My dad would tell me to, 'Play for those who couldn't play.' So my motivation is for people who struggle in life daily."

Kerri Walsh Jennings' Path:

Kerri Walsh Jennings, born on August 15, 1978, in Santa Clara, California, also had a passion for volleyball from a young age. Standing at 6'3", she often felt self-conscious about her height during her childhood. However, she transformed this perceived disadvantage into a strength, becoming a dominant force on the court. Kerri's journey was also marked by battles with self-doubt. She once admitted, "I think a lot of people think that the injuries and the losses have been the hardest part of my career, but the No.1 thing (actually) has been my self-doubt."

The Formation of a Legendary Partnership:

When Misty and Kerri teamed up in 2001, their contrasting personalities and complementary skills created a perfect synergy. Misty's defensive prowess combined with Kerri's offensive strength made them an indomitable pair. Their relationship was built on open communication and unwavering trust. Misty once remarked, "We're a team, and just by the nature of our sport, we're always promoted together. I think we are definitely two different people with two different personalities, but we're always linked."

Overcoming Challenges Together:

Their journey wasn't without obstacles. Both athletes faced injuries and personal setbacks. However, their mutual respect and dedication to each other propelled them forward. Kerri emphasized the importance of continuous self-improvement, stating, "I don't want to be better than you or her or him—I want to be better than I am right now."

Legacy of Trust and Communication:

Misty and Kerri's partnership exemplified the power of collaboration. Their success was not just a result of individual talent but a testament to their collective effort. Misty highlighted the significance of teamwork, saying, "I wouldn't be the best offensive player if I didn't have a great setter. She serves me up nectar."

Their story serves as an inspiration, demonstrating that with trust, communication, and mutual respect, collaborative triumphs are not only possible but can lead to unprecedented success.

Building Trust Within Your Team: The Key to Success in Sports

Trust is the cornerstone of every successful team. It fosters connection, collaboration, and cohesion, empowering athletes to perform at their best both individually and collectively. Without trust, even the most talented teams can struggle to achieve their full potential. Building trust isn't just about creating a positive environment; it's a deliberate and ongoing process that demands intentionality from coaches and players alike.

Why Trust Matters in Teams

Trust creates the foundation for open communication, mutual respect, and shared accountability. When teammates trust one another, they feel safe to take risks, voice their thoughts, and rely on each other during high-pressure situations. For coaches, building trust with their players means creating an environment where feedback is constructive, expectations are clear, and each athlete feels valued.

Without trust, teams often encounter:

- **Communication Breakdowns**: Players may hesitate to speak up or misunderstand each other's intentions.

- **Conflict Escalation**: A lack of trust can exacerbate disagreements and create friction.

- **Reduced Performance**: Players who don't feel supported may struggle to give their best effort.

Teams with strong trust, however, are more resilient, adaptive, and capable of achieving their goals.

Steps to Build Trust Within Your Team

1. Establish Clear Expectations

Trust starts with clarity. Coaches should outline their expectations for behavior, effort, and teamwork early in the season. When players know what's expected of them, they're more likely to hold themselves accountable and trust that others will do the same.

For example:

- Set ground rules for communication, such as using constructive language during feedback.

- Clarify roles and responsibilities so that every player understands how they contribute to the team's success.

2. Lead by Example

As a coach or team leader, your actions set the tone for the group. Demonstrating integrity, consistency, and empathy will encourage your team to do the same.

Ways to lead by example include:

- Following through on commitments.

- Admitting mistakes and showing a willingness to learn.

- Treating every team member with respect, regardless of their skill level.

3. Encourage Open Communication

A team that communicates effectively builds trust more quickly. Create opportunities for players to share their thoughts, concerns, and feedback in a safe and supportive environment.

Strategies to improve communication include:

- Holding regular team meetings where players can voice opinions.

- Encouraging active listening during discussions.

- Using open-ended questions to facilitate dialogue, such as "What do you think we can improve as a team?"

4. Foster Relationships

Trust isn't built in isolation. Encourage teammates to get to know one another beyond the court or field. Strong interpersonal connections enhance trust and teamwork.

Ideas to foster relationships include:

- Team-building activities like group challenges or retreats.

- Celebrating personal milestones, such as birthdays or academic achievements.

- Pairing teammates for practice drills to strengthen bonds.

5. Address Conflict Constructively

Conflict is inevitable, but how it's handled can either strengthen or erode trust. Address disagreements promptly and create a process for resolving them constructively.

Steps to manage conflict effectively:

- Focus on the issue, not the individuals involved.

- Encourage players to express their feelings without assigning blame.

- Collaborate on solutions that satisfy everyone involved.

6. Recognize Effort and Growth

Acknowledging individual and team accomplishments reinforces trust and motivates players to keep improving. Celebrate not only big wins but also small steps toward progress.

Recognition can include:

- Shoutouts during team meetings for exceptional effort.

- Highlighting improvement in specific skills or behaviors.

- Expressing gratitude for players who support their teammates.

Overcoming Challenges in Building Trust

Building trust takes time and effort, and it's not always a smooth process. Setbacks, such as conflicts or mistakes, can challenge a team's trust. However, these moments are opportunities for growth. By addressing issues with honesty and openness, teams can emerge stronger.

For instance, if a player feels excluded or misunderstood, addressing the situation directly and creating space for dialogue can rebuild trust and strengthen relationships.

The Long-Term Benefits of Trust

Teams that prioritize trust enjoy benefits that extend beyond performance. Athletes in trusting environments often report higher levels of satisfaction, reduced stress, and stronger connections with their teammates. These benefits contribute to a positive and sustainable team culture, allowing athletes to grow as both players and individuals.

Conclusion: Trust as the Foundation of Success

Trust isn't just a buzzword—it's the foundation of every successful team. By fostering open communication, demonstrating integrity, and prioritizing relationships, coaches and players can build the kind of trust that turns a group of individuals into a cohesive, high-performing team. With trust as the cornerstone, teams can tackle challenges, celebrate achievements, and reach their full potential together.

Effective Communication on the Court

Misty May-Treanor and Kerri Walsh Jennings mastered the art of on-court communication, an essential element in their unparalleled success as a beach volleyball duo. Their ability to seamlessly coordinate plays was rooted in both verbal and non-verbal cues that fostered trust and clarity in high-pressure situations.

Verbal Communication: Misty and Kerri developed a shorthand of key phrases and terms to keep their exchanges efficient and direct during matches. Whether calling out the opponent's positioning or signaling a change in strategy, their communication was concise and purposeful. "We trusted each other completely," Kerri explained in an interview. "If she called a play, I didn't second-guess it—I just went for it." This immediate trust in their words allowed them to act quickly and decisively, even under intense pressure.

Non-Verbal Communication: In addition to spoken cues, Misty and Kerri relied heavily on non-verbal signals. Subtle gestures, eye contact, and body language became integral to their coordination. For instance, during serves, Misty would flash quick hand signals behind her back to indicate strategy, while Kerri would nod in silent acknowledgment before executing their plan. This fluid communication style minimized misunderstandings and kept their focus sharp.

The Result: Their mastery of communication allowed them to adapt to opponents' strategies mid-game and maintain a unified front. Whether they were defending a spike or setting up a perfect play, their verbal and non-verbal cues worked in harmony, creating a rhythm that their competitors struggled to disrupt. Their ability to remain in sync, even in the most intense matches, highlighted the importance of communication in achieving team cohesion.

Conflict Resolution Strategies for Teams

No partnership is without its challenges, and Misty and Kerri's journey was no exception. Despite their remarkable success, they occasionally faced differences in opinion and external pressures. However, their approach to resolving conflicts constructively became a cornerstone of their partnership.

Addressing Issues Early: Both athletes believed in tackling problems head-on rather than letting tensions build. If disagreements arose during practice or matches, they made a point of addressing them immediately. "We were always honest with each other," Misty shared. "We didn't let things fester—we talked it out and moved forward." By prioritizing open dialogue, they prevented small issues from escalating into larger conflicts.

Focusing on the Goal: Misty and Kerri's shared commitment to winning kept them united even during moments of discord. Whenever emotions ran high, they reminded themselves of their mutual goal: to be the best team in the world. This perspective helped them shift their focus from individual frustrations to the bigger picture, reinforcing their partnership.

Leveraging Their Differences: Their contrasting personalities—Misty's calm demeanor and Kerri's fiery intensity—could have clashed, but instead, they learned to see these differences as assets. Misty's steady presence balanced Kerri's high energy, and Kerri's passion often reignited Misty's drive during tough matches. By valuing each other's unique strengths, they turned potential conflicts into opportunities for growth.

The Role of Mutual Respect: At the heart of their conflict resolution was deep respect for one another. They acknowledged each other's contributions and refrained from personal criticism, focusing instead on constructive feedback. This mutual respect fostered an environment where they could express themselves without fear of judgment.

The Outcome: By navigating challenges with honesty, respect, and a shared vision, Misty and Kerri maintained a strong and cohesive partnership. Their ability to resolve conflicts constructively not only preserved their relationship but also strengthened their performance as a team. This approach contributed significantly to their legendary status, proving that overcoming challenges together is key to long-term success.

Misty May-Treanor and Kerri Walsh Jennings' story is a testament to the power of effective communication and conflict resolution. Their ability to coordinate seamlessly on the court and address challenges constructively off it was instrumental in their journey to becoming one of the greatest teams in sports history. Their example inspires athletes everywhere to prioritize trust, communication, and mutual respect to achieve both personal and collective greatness.

Reflection and Growth Worksheet

Use this worksheet to reflect on and apply the lessons from each chapter. Players and coaches can use these prompts individually or in team discussions to enhance learning and performance.

- What qualities make a strong team?

- Write down one thing you admire about each teammate and how it contributes to the team's success.

- Reflect on a time when your team struggled with communication. How could it have been handled better?

- List three ways you can help build trust within your team.

Chapter 6

Navigating Parental and Coaching Relationships

Gabrielle "Gabby" Reece stood on the sand, her bare feet digging into the warm grains of Hermosa Beach. The familiar sounds of seagulls overhead and the rhythmic crash of waves against the shore should have been calming, but today they weren't. Gabby was in the middle of one of the hardest stretches of her career. The media was scrutinizing her performance, and the weight of her own expectations felt suffocating. On top of that, her team's recent losses had shaken her confidence, leaving her questioning if she could continue competing at the elite level she had worked so hard to reach.

It was during this time that Gabby turned to the people she trusted most—her close-knit support system. Her husband, professional surfer Laird Hamilton, was her rock. Laird had always been her voice of reason, grounding her when the pressures of being a professional athlete seemed too overwhelming. "You're so much more than your wins and losses, Gabby," he told her one evening as they sat on their back porch, watching the Pacific Ocean dissolve into the sunset. The golden light bathed them in warmth, but it was Laird's steady presence that truly made

Gabby feel safe. "Focus on what you can control. You've faced bigger waves than this, and you've always found a way through."

Gabby also leaned on her coach, a straight-talking mentor who had seen her through countless highs and lows. After a particularly grueling practice session, where Gabby's spikes lacked their usual power and her frustration bubbled to the surface, her coach pulled her aside. "What's going on, Gabby?" he asked, his voice calm but firm.

"I don't know," she admitted, slumping onto a bench as she wiped sweat from her brow. "I feel like I've lost my edge. Everyone's expecting so much from me, and I don't know if I can deliver."

Her coach crouched down to her eye level, his expression softening. "Let me tell you something I've learned about you," he said. "You're the toughest competitor I've ever coached—not because you're perfect, but because you don't give up. You've hit walls before, and every time, you've found a way to climb over them. Trust yourself, and trust the people who believe in you."

His words stuck with her, echoing in her mind during sleepless nights and early-morning workouts. It wasn't just encouragement—it was a reminder of her resilience and the foundation of trust she had built with her coach and her teammates.

One pivotal moment came during a crucial tournament match. Gabby's team was down by several points, and the pressure to perform weighed heavily on her shoulders. As the opposing team served, her heart pounded like a drum, her inner voice threatening to drown out her focus. But then, she caught Laird's gaze in the crowd. He wasn't yelling or gesturing wildly; he was simply there, calm and steady, silently reminding her of everything she was capable of.

Her coach's voice broke through the din of the crowd, yelling, "Focus on the next point, not the last!" Gabby nodded, inhaling deeply to reset. When the next ball came her way, she jumped, spiking it with all the force and precision she could muster. The ball thundered into the sand, and the crowd erupted.

Point by point, she clawed her way back, not just on the scoreboard but in her mindset. The match ended with a win, but more importantly, it reignited Gabby's belief in herself. As she embraced her teammates, she looked toward her husband and coach, her heart swelling with gratitude for the people who had stood by her when she needed them most.

That moment encapsulated the power of her support system. It wasn't just about their words or actions—it was about how they made her feel seen, valued, and capable, even in her darkest moments. Gabby later reflected, "I've learned to lean on the people who love me. They remind me that I'm not alone in this journey, and that's what keeps me going."

Gabby's story is a powerful reminder that even the most accomplished athletes need a strong network to navigate the inevitable challenges. For her, the unwavering presence of her husband, the guidance of her coach, and the camaraderie of her teammates provided the foundation she needed to rise above self-doubt and thrive. It's a testament to the strength we can draw from those who believe in us, especially when we struggle to believe in ourselves.

Understanding Parental Expectations: Gabrielle's Balancing Act

Gabrielle Reece's journey to athletic greatness wasn't just shaped by her coaches and teammates; her parents also played a crucial role in her development. However, like many young athletes, Gabby faced the challenge of balancing parental expectations with her own dreams and ambitions. It required self-awareness, communication, and, most importantly, an understanding of her own boundaries.

Gabby's upbringing wasn't conventional. Raised by her mother in the U.S. Virgin Islands, Gabby's father passed away when she was only five years old. Her mother, a single parent, instilled in her a deep sense of independence and resilience. Yet, as Gabby's volleyball talent became apparent, her mother's high expectations also added pressure. "My mom always wanted the best for me," Gabby shared in an interview. "But she also had strong opinions about what that 'best' looked like."

In high school, Gabby's height and athleticism made her a standout player. Her mother encouraged her to use her natural abilities to excel in sports, but Gabby often felt the weight of wanting to live up to those expectations while also pursuing her own goals. "I didn't want to just meet her standards—I wanted to find my own path and succeed on my terms," she later reflected.

Navigating Ambition and Support

Gabby's approach to balancing her mother's support with her ambitions was rooted in communication. She learned to express her aspirations clearly, even when they didn't align perfectly with her mother's vision. For example, when it came time to choose a college, Gabby faced conflicting emotions. Her mother envisioned a future where Gabby prioritized academics and leveraged her volleyball talent for a stable career, while Gabby dreamed of playing professionally and leaving a legacy in the sport.

"I had to explain that volleyball wasn't just a means to an end for me—it was my passion," Gabby shared. "That conversation wasn't easy, but it brought us closer. Once she understood my perspective, she became my biggest cheerleader."

Setting Boundaries

As Gabby progressed in her career, she also learned to set boundaries to maintain a healthy relationship with her family. While she valued her mother's guidance, she recognized the importance of making decisions that aligned with her own vision.

One example came during her professional career when Gabby faced a grueling training schedule and media commitments. Her mother, concerned about her daughter's well-being, urged her to scale back and take more time for herself. While Gabby appreciated the concern, she felt strongly about maintaining her momentum. "I had to tell her, 'I know it's intense, but this is what I need to do right now.'" By framing her decision as a reflection of her goals rather than a rejection of her mother's advice, Gabby struck a balance that honored both perspectives.

Lessons for Athletes and Parents

Gabby's experience highlights the delicate balance between parental support and personal ambition. For young athletes, her story underscores the importance of:

- **Open Communication**: Honest discussions about goals and expectations can prevent misunderstandings and foster mutual respect.

- **Self-Advocacy**: Athletes should feel empowered to express their ambitions, even when they differ from parental expectations.

- **Setting Boundaries**: Establishing limits ensures that relationships remain supportive rather than overbearing.

For parents, Gabby's story serves as a reminder to:

- **Listen Actively**: Understand your child's aspirations and recognize that their path may differ from your own vision.

- **Offer Encouragement Without Pressure**: Provide guidance while allowing your child the freedom to make their own choices.

- **Celebrate Their Journey**: Acknowledge progress and growth, regardless of the outcome.

The Takeaway

Gabby's ability to navigate her mother's expectations while staying true to her own goals played a vital role in her success. It wasn't always easy, but by fostering mutual understanding and setting clear boundaries, she created a foundation of support that fueled her ambitions. Her story is a testament to the power of open communication and the importance of balancing external expectations with personal dreams.

Mastering Coach-to-Athlete Communication: A Guide for Young Volleyball Players

Effective communication between a coach and athlete is one of the most important elements of success in sports, especially in volleyball. Whether it's calling plays on the court, discussing strategies during practice, or simply building trust, communication can make or break the athlete-coach relationship. Here's how young volleyball players can better understand and embrace strong communication with their coaches to elevate their game and foster a positive team environment.

Why Communication Matters

Good communication is the foundation of any great team. Coaches who communicate effectively help athletes like you:

- Understand expectations and goals.

- Learn how to improve their performance.

- Build confidence and trust on and off the court.

As a volleyball player, knowing how to communicate with your coach can help you clarify your role on the team, get constructive feedback, and even improve team dynamics.

Keys to Effective Coach-Athlete Communication

1. Listen Actively

Communication isn't just about speaking—it's also about listening. When your coach provides instructions or feedback, focus on what they're saying without interrupting or assuming. Show that you're engaged by maintaining eye contact and asking thoughtful questions.

For example, if your coach tells you to adjust your footwork during a spike, you could respond with, "Got it! Should I also focus on my arm swing to improve my angle?"

2. Be Open to Feedback

Constructive criticism is a part of growing as an athlete. It's not always easy to hear, but feedback from your coach is meant to help you improve. Instead of taking it personally, view it as an opportunity to learn.

Remember, even the best players in the world, like Misty May-Treanor and Kerri Walsh Jennings, listened to their coaches to refine their game. When you're open to feedback, you show that you're committed to becoming the best player you can be.

3. Speak Up When Needed

Your coach isn't a mind reader. If you're struggling with a skill, feeling unsure about your role, or dealing with stress, it's important to let them know. Coaches appreciate players who communicate honestly and respectfully.

For instance, if you're finding it hard to keep up with practice drills, you might say, "Coach, I'm having a hard time with this drill. Can you walk me through it again or give me tips to improve?"

4. Use Positive Body Language

Your body language speaks volumes. Slouching, avoiding eye contact, or rolling your eyes can send the wrong message, even if you don't mean it. Instead, practice positive body language by standing tall, nodding when your coach speaks, and showing enthusiasm during practice and games.

Positive body language not only shows respect but also builds trust with your coach and teammates.

5. Build Trust Through Actions

Trust is earned, and it's a two-way street. Show your coach that you're dependable by giving 100% effort during practices and games, being on time, and staying focused. When your coach sees your dedication, they're more likely to trust you with greater responsibilities on the team.

How Coaches Communicate Effectively

While it's important for athletes to communicate well, coaches also have a responsibility to foster strong relationships. Here are some ways coaches work to connect with players like you:

1. Setting Clear Expectations

Coaches often lay out specific goals and rules for the team. When you understand these expectations, it's easier to stay on track and know what's expected of you.

2. Offering Consistent Feedback

Good coaches provide regular feedback, not just during games but also during practice. They point out areas for improvement while celebrating your progress, keeping you motivated.

3. Encouraging Open Dialogue

The best coaches create a space where athletes feel comfortable speaking up. They welcome questions, listen to concerns, and value the opinions of their players.

Bridging the Gap: Tips for Better Communication

If you want to strengthen your relationship with your coach, here are a few tips:

- **Practice Respect:** Always approach your coach with a positive and respectful attitude.

- **Ask for Clarification:** If you don't understand something, don't hesitate to ask for further explanation.

- **Stay Calm Under Pressure:** Even in tense moments, keep your composure and focus on solutions.

- **Celebrate Team Successes:** Acknowledge your coach's role in helping the team achieve its goals.

The Power of Communication in Volleyball

Volleyball is a team sport that thrives on communication. From calling out plays to encouraging teammates, your ability to communicate effectively can transform your performance and strengthen your team dynamic. Remember, your coach is there to guide you—not just as a player but as a person.

By embracing open, respectful, and honest communication, you'll not only grow as an athlete but also build a lasting relationship with your coach that can inspire you long after you've left the court.

Finding Your Voice as a Young Volleyball Athlete

As a young volleyball player, you know the importance of teamwork, practice, and determination. But have you ever thought about the power of your voice? Speaking up, sharing your thoughts, and advocating for yourself are just as important as mastering your serves and spikes. Finding your voice isn't always easy, especially when surrounded by experienced coaches and teammates. But learning to express yourself can transform your game and your confidence.

Here's how you can find and use your voice effectively as a young volleyball athlete.

Why Your Voice Matters on the Court

Volleyball is a fast-paced, communication-heavy sport. Your voice plays a critical role in:

- **Building Trust with Teammates:** Calling the ball or encouraging a teammate creates connection and ensures smooth teamwork.

- **Improving Team Strategy:** Sharing insights, like spotting an opponent's weak spot, can give your team an edge.

- **Strengthening Your Confidence:** When you speak up, you show that you're engaged and ready to lead.

Being vocal also shows your coach that you're serious about your growth, which can open up more opportunities for leadership on and off the court.

How to Find Your Voice

1. Start Small

If speaking up feels intimidating, begin with small, manageable steps. For example, during practice, try calling out, "Mine!" when going for a ball or saying, "Great pass!" to a teammate. These small interactions help build your confidence and show your team that you're paying attention.

2. Ask Questions

If you don't understand a drill or strategy, don't hesitate to ask your coach for clarification. Questions like, "Should I adjust my positioning here?" or "Can you explain that play again?" show that you're invested in learning. Coaches appreciate athletes who are eager to improve and willing to engage.

3. Give Feedback (and Accept It Too)

Finding your voice doesn't just mean speaking—it also means listening. If a teammate asks for your opinion or feedback, offer it in a positive, constructive way. At the same time, be open to feedback from others. A strong team thrives on mutual respect and clear communication.

4. Practice Outside the Game

Sometimes, the best way to build confidence is outside the heat of competition. Talk with your coach or teammates during downtime. Share your thoughts, ask for advice, or discuss how you can improve. These casual conversations can make speaking up during games feel more natural.

Overcoming Common Challenges

Finding your voice can be tough, especially when you feel shy, fear judgment, or worry about making mistakes. Here's how to push past those challenges:

- **Fear of Judgment:** Remember, everyone on your team is working toward the same goal. Your teammates and coach want you to succeed, and they'll respect you for contributing your ideas.

- **Mistakes Happen:** It's okay to be wrong sometimes. Mistakes are part of learning, and showing that you're willing to take risks helps build trust with your team.

- **Shyness:** If speaking up feels hard, try writing down what you want to say before practice or games. Rehearsing your thoughts can make them easier to express when the time comes.

Using Your Voice to Lead

Being vocal isn't just about being loud—it's about leading with confidence and purpose. Here's how you can use your voice to lead as a volleyball player:

- **Encourage Teammates:** A simple "You've got this!" can lift someone's spirits during a tough match.

- **Communicate Strategies:** Be clear and concise when calling plays or pointing out an opponent's weaknesses.

- **Take Initiative:** If you notice something that could help your team, like adjusting positioning or focusing on defense, share it.

Your Voice, Your Power

Finding your voice is about more than just volleyball—it's about becoming a confident, empowered person both on and off the court. By practicing clear communication, building trust with your team, and overcoming fears, you'll discover the power of your voice and its ability to inspire, connect, and lead.

So next time you step on the court, don't just bring your skills—bring your voice, too. It could be the key to unlocking your full potential as an athlete and teammate.

Reflection and Growth Worksheet

Use this worksheet to reflect on and apply the lessons from each chapter. Players and coaches can use these prompts individually or in team discussions to enhance learning and performance.

- What expectations do you feel from your parents or coaches?

- How can you communicate your goals and needs effectively to your parents or coach?

- Reflect on a moment when a coach or parent supported you positively. How did it help?

- Write down one boundary you want to establish with a parent or coach and why it's important.

Chapter 7

Developing Resilience and Coping Mechanisms

From the dusty streets of Dashoguz, Turkmenistan, where the laughter of children filled the air, a young boy named Ibragim began a journey that would redefine resilience. In a neighborhood where makeshift games brought the community together, Ibragim was impossible to miss—his boundless energy and love for sports set him apart. But it wasn't just his athleticism that drew attention; it was his unshakable enthusiasm, a spark that hinted at the remarkable story yet to unfold.

However, life took an unexpected turn when, as a young adult working at a train station, Ibragim was involved in a devastating car accident that resulted in the loss of his foot. The once active and spirited individual found himself confined to a hospital bed, grappling with the physical pain and the emotional turmoil of his new reality. The weight of a 6 kg iron prosthesis added to his burden, making every step a painful reminder of what he had lost.

"People would stare at me while I walked down the street. I could not accept the fact that I was now a person with a disability," Ibragim recalls.

Determined not to be defined by his disability, Ibragim sought better prosthetic solutions in Ashgabat, the capital city. There, he encountered two coaches who introduced him to a sports club for individuals with disabilities. This marked the beginning of his transformation.

"It was hard at first. I fell down, but I stood up," he shares, reflecting on his early days at the club.

Through perseverance, he not only adapted but thrived, eventually returning to Dashoguz to coach volleyball, barbell, and table tennis for people with disabilities.

Under Ibragim's guidance, nearly 60 students have found purpose and community through sports. He recounts the transformative journey of Hushnur, who, through rigorous training, moved from reliance on crutches to playing tennis for two hours straight. Ibragim's dream is to elevate his students to the international stage, particularly the Paralympic Games, as he steps into the role of a senior coach in the sport of sitting volleyball.

Ibragim's story is a powerful reminder that adversity can be a catalyst for profound personal growth. His journey from despair to empowerment underscores the importance of resilience, community support, and the belief that we are, indeed, different but equal.

Building Mental Toughness Through Adversity

Ibragim's journey from tragedy to triumph is a masterclass in building mental toughness. Losing his foot in a devastating accident could have ended his aspirations, but instead, it became the turning point that defined his character. His resilience and determination turned what seemed like insurmountable obstacles into opportunities for growth, setting an example for others to follow.

Facing the Reality of Loss

After his accident, Ibragim faced one of his greatest challenges: coming to terms with his new reality. The initial days were filled with doubt, pain, and the emotional toll of accepting life with a disability. He was no longer the same agile and athletic person who had run freely across fields. Yet, in these moments of despair, Ibragim made a conscious decision. Rather than allowing his circumstances to control his future, he chose to rebuild his life.

"I knew I couldn't go back to who I was before, but I also realized that didn't mean I couldn't become something just as good—or even better," he reflected.

Turning Challenges into Opportunities

1. Seeking Support

Instead of isolating himself, Ibragim sought help. His journey to Ashgabat to find better prosthetics was his first step toward reclaiming his independence. More importantly, it introduced him to a supportive community of athletes with disabilities. By surrounding himself with individuals who shared similar struggles, Ibragim realized he was not alone—and this newfound sense of camaraderie fueled his determination to succeed.

2. Embracing Sports as a Catalyst for Growth

Ibragim's entry into the sports club in Ashgabat was transformative. At first, simply participating in activities like volleyball felt daunting. His prosthetic leg was heavy, and his movements were awkward. He fell frequently, often in front of others. But every fall became an opportunity to stand back up.

"I learned to fall, and I learned to rise again," he said. "That's when I realized that every failure was just another chance to improve."

Through countless hours of practice, Ibragim not only regained physical strength but also built a mental toughness that allowed him to push through discomfort and frustration. Each small victory, whether it was completing a drill or lasting longer in a match, reaffirmed his belief in his ability to adapt and grow.

3. Shifting Perspective

One of Ibragim's most profound shifts was in how he viewed his disability. What once felt like a limitation became a source of strength and inspiration. Instead of focusing on what he couldn't do, Ibragim embraced what he could achieve—and how he could inspire others. This mental shift was a cornerstone in building his resilience.

Becoming a Role Model

Ibragim's mental toughness wasn't just about overcoming his own challenges; it was about helping others do the same. When he returned to Dashoguz to coach athletes with disabilities, he brought with him the lessons he had learned through his struggles. He understood the doubts and fears his students faced because he had lived them himself.

As a coach, Ibragim created an environment that encouraged growth through adversity. He taught his athletes that their setbacks didn't define them. Instead, he emphasized the importance of perseverance, celebrating small victories, and learning from failures.

One of his students, Hushnur, was initially hesitant to even attempt physical activity, relying heavily on crutches. Ibragim pushed him gently but firmly, reminding him that progress came one step at a time. Over months of consistent training, Hushnur transformed. He eventually played table tennis for hours without needing crutches—a testament to both his hard work and Ibragim's mentorship.

Mental Toughness as a Way of Life

Ibragim's ability to transform his challenges into opportunities is rooted in a simple yet powerful mindset: the belief that growth comes through perseverance. His story teaches young athletes, especially those facing their own adversities, that mental toughness isn't about being invincible. It's about rising every time you fall, learning from your mistakes, and embracing the journey, no matter how difficult it may seem.

As Ibragim puts it, "We are all different, but we are equal. And in that difference, we find our strength."

Through his resilience and determination, Ibragim has shown that adversity is not the end of the story—it's the beginning of something extraordinary.

Coping with Losses and Setbacks

Ibragim's life has been a series of challenges, from losing his foot to navigating the emotional and physical setbacks that followed. His ability to process these difficulties and move forward offers valuable lessons for athletes who face their own losses.

Acknowledging the Setback

The first step in Ibragim's recovery was recognizing the weight of his loss. He didn't ignore the pain or frustration—instead, he allowed himself to feel it. "At first, I wanted to pretend everything was fine, but I learned that ignoring it didn't help. I had to face it head-on," he said. By acknowledging the reality of his situation, Ibragim was able to begin the healing process.

For young athletes, this means understanding that setbacks—whether they're injuries, losses, or missed opportunities—are part of the journey. It's okay to feel disappointed or frustrated, but it's important to not let those emotions consume you.

Focusing on the Next Step

Rather than dwelling on what he couldn't do, Ibragim focused on what was within his control. Whether it was practicing his balance with his prosthesis or learning new skills at the sports club, each small step forward helped him rebuild confidence and momentum.

For athletes coping with setbacks, breaking the recovery process into manageable goals can make it feel less overwhelming. Celebrate small victories, like regaining strength or mastering a specific skill, to remind yourself of your progress.

Leaning on Support Systems

Ibragim's journey highlights the importance of community. His coaches, teammates, and family members provided emotional and practical support, encouraging him to persevere. When setbacks felt too heavy to bear alone, their encouragement kept him grounded and motivated.

For young athletes, reaching out to trusted mentors, teammates, or family members can make a huge difference during tough times. You don't have to face setbacks alone.

Strategies for Injury Recovery

Recovering from an injury or major setback isn't just about physical rehabilitation—it's also a mental battle. Ibragim's ability to stay engaged with his sport during his recovery offers a blueprint for athletes navigating similar challenges.

1. Maintaining a Positive Mindset

After his accident, Ibragim struggled with self-doubt and frustration. To combat these feelings, he focused on maintaining a positive outlook. "Every day, I reminded myself that progress was possible, even if it was slow," he shared. Visualization became a key tool—he would imagine himself playing volleyball, moving fluidly despite his prosthesis, and succeeding in ways he hadn't thought possible.

For recovering athletes, visualization can be a powerful way to stay mentally connected to your sport. Picture yourself performing at your best, even if you're temporarily sidelined, to reinforce your belief in your ability to return.

2. Staying Connected to the Sport

Even during the early stages of his recovery, Ibragim stayed involved in volleyball. He attended games and practices, observing strategies and cheering on teammates. This helped him stay engaged with the sport he loved and kept his passion alive.

Young athletes recovering from injuries can find similar ways to stay involved. Watching games, studying strategies, or helping teammates with drills can keep you mentally sharp and connected to your team.

3. Practicing Patience

One of the hardest lessons Ibragim learned was the importance of patience. Recovery wasn't linear—there were good days and bad days, and progress often felt slow. However, by focusing on long-term goals rather than immediate results, he was able to stay motivated.

For athletes, accepting that recovery takes time is crucial. Focus on what you can do each day to improve, and trust the process.

4. Finding New Purpose

Perhaps the most transformative part of Ibragim's recovery was his decision to coach. Helping others discover their potential, despite their physical challenges, gave him a renewed sense of purpose and a deeper connection to volleyball. "Coaching reminded me that my journey could inspire others," he said.

If you're recovering from an injury, consider exploring new roles within your sport. Coaching, mentoring, or even learning about the game from a different perspective can give you a fresh sense of purpose.

A Legacy of Resilience

Ibragim's story is a powerful reminder that setbacks, no matter how significant, don't have to define your future. By processing his losses, leaning on his support system, and finding purpose in helping others, he turned adversity into opportunity. For young athletes, his journey highlights the importance of perseverance, patience, and a positive mindset.

Whether you're facing an injury, a tough loss, or a personal challenge, remember Ibragim's words: "You may fall, but you can always rise again." With resilience and determination, there's no limit to what you can achieve.

Reflection and Growth Worksheet

Use this worksheet to reflect on and apply the lessons from each chapter. Players and coaches can use these prompts individually or in team discussions to enhance learning and performance.

7. Developing Resilience and Coping Mechanisms

* What is the biggest adversity you've faced in volleyball? How did you overcome it?

* Write down three ways you can turn setbacks into opportunities for growth.

* List two strategies to stay motivated during tough times, like injuries or losing streaks.

* Reflect on how you stay connected to the sport when you're unable to play (e.g., during recovery or offseason).

Chapter 8

The Importance of Nutrition and the Mind

Volleyball is a sport of agility, speed, and precision. Whether diving for a save, spiking the ball, or sprinting to cover the court, young volleyball players need peak physical and mental performance. Nutrition, often overlooked, is the cornerstone of this performance. It's not just about eating to stay full; it's about fueling your body to excel, recover, and thrive both on and off the court.

In this chapter, we'll dive into the importance of nutrition for young volleyball players, exploring the key nutrients, hydration strategies, timing of meals, and actionable tips to build a performance-enhancing diet.

Why Nutrition Matters in Volleyball

The Demands of the Game

Volleyball is a high-intensity sport that requires short bursts of energy, quick reflexes, and sustained focus. Players must jump, sprint, and dive repeatedly during matches and practices. This places unique demands on the body:

- **Energy**: The anaerobic bursts of energy required for spiking, blocking, and sprinting rely on carbohydrate stores.

- **Strength**: Building and maintaining muscle strength for explosive movements depends on adequate protein intake.

- **Endurance**: Stamina for long matches requires balanced nutrition that sustains energy over time.

- **Focus**: Mental clarity and decision-making are essential for strategic plays and require steady blood sugar levels.

Building a Strong Foundation

Young athletes are not only fueling their sports performance but also supporting growth and development. Proper nutrition ensures:

- Strong bones and reduced risk of injuries.

- Optimal muscle development and repair.

- A robust immune system to fight off illness.

The Key Nutrients for Volleyball Players

1. Carbohydrates: The Primary Energy Source

Carbohydrates are the fuel that powers every sprint, jump, and dive on the court. They are stored as glycogen in the muscles and liver, ready to be used during intense activity.

- **Sources**: Whole grains (brown rice, quinoa, whole-wheat bread), fruits (bananas, apples, berries), starchy vegetables (sweet potatoes, corn), and dairy products (milk, yogurt).

- **Timing**: Aim for a carb-rich meal 3-4 hours before practice or a game and a smaller snack 30-60 minutes prior for quick energy.

- **Post-Game**: Replenish glycogen stores within 30 minutes of play with easily digestible carbs like fruit or a sports drink.

2. Protein: Building and Repairing Muscle

Protein is essential for muscle recovery and growth, particularly for young athletes undergoing training and physical development.

- **Sources**: Lean meats (chicken, turkey), fish, eggs, dairy (Greek yogurt, cottage cheese), plant-based proteins (tofu, lentils, beans), and nuts.

- **Timing**: Incorporate protein into every meal, especially within two hours after exercise to support muscle repair.

- **Portions**: A palm-sized serving of protein is a good guideline for each meal.

3. Healthy Fats: Sustained Energy

Fats provide a longer-lasting energy source and are essential for brain function and hormone production.

- **Sources**: Avocados, nuts, seeds, fatty fish (salmon, mackerel), and oils (olive oil, flaxseed oil).

- **Moderation**: Focus on unsaturated fats and avoid trans fats or excessive saturated fats found in processed foods.

4. Vitamins and Minerals: The Unsung Heroes

Vitamins and minerals support everything from energy production to immune function and bone health.

- **Calcium**: Builds strong bones and prevents stress fractures. Found in dairy, leafy greens, and fortified plant-based milks.

- **Iron**: Transports oxygen in the blood, vital for endurance. Found in lean red meat, beans, and spinach.

- **Vitamin D**: Aids in calcium absorption and muscle function. Found in fortified foods and sunlight exposure.

- **Electrolytes (Sodium, Potassium, Magnesium)**: Prevent cramping and maintain hydration. Found in bananas, nuts, and sports drinks.

5. Hydration: The Lifeline of Performance

Dehydration can lead to fatigue, cramps, and reduced performance. Young athletes must stay ahead of their hydration needs.

- **Water**: Essential for maintaining body temperature and supporting metabolism.

- **Electrolytes**: During intense or long sessions, sports drinks can replenish lost electrolytes.

- **Guidelines**: Drink water consistently throughout the day. Aim for 16-20 ounces two hours before practice, 7-10 ounces every 20 minutes during exercise, and 16-24 ounces for every pound lost after activity.

The Role of Nutrition Timing

Pre-Game Nutrition

Fueling up before games ensures athletes have the energy to perform at their best.

- **3-4 Hours Before**: Eat a balanced meal with carbs, protein, and a small amount of fat. Example: Grilled chicken with quinoa and roasted vegetables.

- **30-60 Minutes Before**: Choose a light, carb-focused snack. Example: A banana with a tablespoon of almond butter.

During Games and Practices

Sustaining energy during long matches or intense practices is crucial.

- **Quick Fuel**: Sports drinks, fruit, or energy gels can provide a quick carb boost.

- **Hydration**: Sip water or electrolyte drinks regularly to stay hydrated.

Post-Game Recovery

The recovery window is critical for repairing muscles and replenishing energy.

- **Within 30 Minutes**: Consume carbs and protein. Example: Chocolate milk or a smoothie with fruit and protein powder.

- **Within 2 Hours**: Eat a balanced meal with carbs, protein, and vegetables. Example: Salmon with sweet potatoes and steamed broccoli.

Common Pitfalls and How to Avoid Them

1. Skipping Meals

Skipping meals can lead to low energy levels, reduced performance, and slower recovery. Plan ahead to ensure meals are prepared and ready, even on busy days.

2. Relying on Junk Food

While tempting, sugary snacks and fast food can lead to energy crashes and poor long-term health. Opt for whole, nutrient-dense options instead.

3. Underestimating Hydration

Many young athletes don't drink enough water. Keep a water bottle handy and make hydration a habit.

4. Ignoring Individual Needs

Every athlete is different. Some may require more calories, while others need to focus on specific nutrients. Listen to your body and consult a nutritionist if needed.

Practical Tips for Young Volleyball Players

1. **Meal Prep**: Prepare meals and snacks in advance to avoid skipping or resorting to unhealthy options.

2. **Snack Smart**: Keep portable, healthy snacks like trail mix, granola bars, or fruit in your bag for quick energy.

3. **Experiment**: Test different foods during practice to see what works best for your body.

4. **Track Your Intake**: Use a journal or app to track meals, hydration, and energy levels to find patterns and improve performance.

Real-Life Example: Kerri Walsh Jennings

Kerri Walsh Jennings, a three-time Olympic gold medalist in beach volleyball, emphasizes the importance of nutrition in her training. "What you put in your body directly impacts your performance. I focus on eating clean, whole foods to fuel my body and mind," she said. Her diet includes lean proteins, vegetables, and healthy fats, and she prioritizes hydration to keep her energy high during grueling matches.

Conclusion: Fuel Your Success

Nutrition isn't just about eating—it's about empowering yourself to perform at your best. By focusing on balanced meals, proper hydration, and strategic timing, young volleyball players can unlock their full potential on the court. Remember, every bite you take is an investment in your game, your health, and your future. Take the lessons from this chapter and start fueling for success today.

Reflection and Growth Worksheet

Use this worksheet to reflect on and apply the lessons from each chapter. Players and coaches can use these prompts individually or in team discussions to enhance learning and performance.

- How does your current diet impact your performance?

- List three foods or habits you can incorporate to fuel

your body and mind better.

- Reflect on a time when proper nutrition or hydration improved your game. What did you learn?

- Create a sample pre-game and post-game meal plan that supports your performance and recovery.

Chapter 9

Drills for Success

Building Mental Toughness with Volleyball Drills: In-Depth Guide

Mental toughness is the edge that separates good volleyball players from great ones. It's about staying composed under pressure, bouncing back from mistakes, and maintaining focus even when fatigue sets in. Specific volleyball drills can be designed not only to enhance physical performance but also to cultivate the mental resilience needed to excel in high-pressure scenarios.

Here's a detailed breakdown of drills designed to develop mental toughness, complete with step-by-step setups, goals, and pacing to ensure effectiveness.

1. Pressure Serving Drill

Setup:
- Divide the team into two groups or allow individual players to compete against themselves.

- Mark a target zone on the court, such as specific corners or areas within the service box.

- Players start with zero points, and each successful serve earns one point.

Execution:
- The goal is to reach a predetermined score (e.g., 10 points).

- A successful serve that lands in the target zone earns a point.

- A missed serve resets the player's score to zero.

- Increase the difficulty by introducing pressure elements, such as a countdown clock or simulated game situations.

Pace: Allow players 10-15 seconds between serves to simulate game pacing. Emphasize a steady rhythm and remind players to take deep breaths before each attempt.

Mental Toughness Focus: This drill mimics the high-pressure environment of serving at a critical game moment. Players learn to manage anxiety, trust their skills, and focus on execution without dwelling on the consequences of failure.

2. Controlled Chaos Drill

Setup:
- The coach stands at the center of the court with multiple volleyballs.

- Divide players into two teams and position them in their standard rotations.

- The coach randomly tosses balls to different areas, forcing players to adjust and react.

Execution:
- Players must maintain communication and make quick decisions to keep the ball in play.

- The coach can increase difficulty by calling out sudden changes, such as requiring a specific player to make the play or restricting the number of allowed touches.

- To add more chaos, the coach can toss multiple balls into play at once.

Pace: Keep the drill fast-paced and unpredictable, with minimal downtime between plays. Run for 3-5 minutes per round, with brief breaks for feedback and adjustment.

Mental Toughness Focus: This drill sharpens players' focus and decision-making in unpredictable situations. It encourages adaptability and effective communication, even when the game feels chaotic.

3. Mistake Recovery Drill

Setup:
- Create a controlled scrimmage or drill that challenges players' defensive skills.

- For example, set up a coach or player to spike balls into

the defensive zone at varying angles and speeds.

Execution:
- Players are expected to dive or react quickly to save the ball. Mistakes are inevitable due to the difficulty.

- After each mistake, players immediately reset and prepare for the next play.

- Incorporate positive reinforcement by encouraging players to acknowledge the mistake briefly, then focus on their next opportunity.

Pace: Keep the pace steady, with balls delivered every 5-7 seconds to give players time to recover and reset mentally.

Mental Toughness Focus: This drill emphasizes the importance of resilience and moving on from errors. It conditions players to view mistakes as learning opportunities rather than setbacks.

4. Focused Rally Drill

Setup:
- Two teams play a controlled rally with the sole goal of keeping the ball in play as long as possible.

- Use cones or markers to create a slightly smaller playing area to increase difficulty.

Execution:
- Teams aim to achieve a specific number of consecutive touches (e.g., 50 touches).

- If the ball drops, the count resets, and the teams must start over.

- Encourage players to communicate continuously and maintain steady, controlled plays rather than aiming for aggressive hits.

Pace: Run this drill for 10-15 minutes, encouraging players to push themselves each round to exceed their previous rally count.

Mental Toughness Focus: This drill builds patience, concentration, and teamwork. The repetitive nature requires players to maintain focus over an extended period, mirroring long, high-stakes rallies in a match.

5. Fatigue Training Drill

Setup:

- Set up a circuit with physically demanding activities, such as sprints, burpees, or box jumps, near the volleyball court.

- Include volleyball-specific tasks, such as spiking, serving, or setting.

Execution:

- Players complete a set of physical exercises (e.g., 20-second sprint followed by 10 burpees).

- Immediately transition to a volleyball task, such as executing five precise serves or blocking five consecutive spikes.

* Cycle through different stations for 3-5 minutes per round.

Pace: Keep transitions quick, with minimal rest between exercises. Allow a 1-minute break between rounds for hydration and regrouping.

Mental Toughness Focus: This drill simulates the mental and physical exhaustion players experience during long matches. It trains athletes to maintain precision and focus, even when fatigued.

6. Silent Communication Drill

Setup:

* Divide the team into two groups and assign them to their usual positions on the court.

* Prohibit verbal communication during plays. Players must rely on eye contact, body language, and intuitive understanding to coordinate.

Execution:

* Conduct a standard scrimmage or drill without allowing players to speak.

* Players must develop alternative methods to signal intentions, such as using hand gestures or pointing.

* Debrief after each round to discuss what worked and what didn't.

Pace: Run the drill in 5-minute rounds, gradually increasing complexity (e.g., adding restrictions on hand gestures or requiring specific plays).

Mental Toughness Focus: This drill improves non-verbal communication and builds trust between teammates. It teaches players to stay calm and connected under pressure.

7. Match Simulation Drill

Setup:

- Divide players into teams and create a game-like scenario, complete with scorekeeping and timeouts.

- Simulate high-pressure situations, such as defending a match point or coming back from a significant deficit.

Execution:

- Coaches can interrupt gameplay to introduce challenges, such as sudden lineup changes or unexpected penalties.

- Players must adapt and execute strategies to overcome the imposed obstacles.

- Emphasize the importance of staying composed and focused on the team's goals.

Pace: Run the simulation as a full set, encouraging players to treat it with the same intensity as a real match.

Mental Toughness Focus: This drill acclimates players to high-pressure scenarios, helping them build confidence and composure for real matches.

8. Visualization and Breathing Practice

Setup:
- Gather players in a quiet space with minimal distractions.

- Provide a brief explanation of the visualization exercise and guide them through a series of controlled breathing techniques.

Execution:
- Players close their eyes and visualize themselves performing successfully on the court, such as executing a perfect spike or making a critical save.

- Encourage them to use all their senses—hearing the crowd, feeling the ball, and seeing the play unfold.

- Incorporate deep breathing exercises, such as inhaling for 4 counts, holding for 4 counts, and exhaling for 6 counts.

Pace: Dedicate 5-10 minutes to this exercise before or after practice.

Mental Toughness Focus: Visualization and breathing practices enhance mental clarity, reduce anxiety, and build confidence by reinforcing positive imagery.

Conclusion

Incorporating these drills into your training routine can help you cultivate the mental toughness needed to succeed in volleyball. By simulating high-pressure scenarios, encouraging resilience after mistakes, and fostering focus during fatigue, you can strengthen both your physical and mental game. Remember, mental toughness is a skill, and like any skill, it improves with consistent practice and dedication. Take these drills to heart, and you'll find yourself more prepared to face challenges on and off the court.

Reflection and Growth Worksheet

Use this worksheet to reflect on and apply the lessons from each chapter. Players and coaches can use these prompts individually or in team discussions to enhance learning and performance.

- What volleyball drill challenges you the most, and why?

- Reflect on how mental toughness helps you push through difficult drills.

- List three ways your team can improve communication during chaotic or high-pressure drills.

- Write down a goal for the next time you practice a mentally challenging drill.

Chapter 10

The 7 Mental Secrets of Volleyball: Unlocking Your Peak Performance

Volleyball is a game of precision, power, and teamwork. But beyond the physical skills and strategic plays lies the often-overlooked mental game—a critical factor that can make or break a player's performance. The mental secrets of volleyball go beyond generic advice; they offer actionable strategies to elevate your play and mindset. In this chapter, we'll explore seven transformative mental techniques that help players achieve peak performance, drawing from the unique challenges and subtleties of the sport.

1. The Art of Anticipation: Reading the Game Before It Happens

Great volleyball players seem to have a sixth sense, appearing in the right place at the right time. This ability isn't magic—it's the art of anticipation, a mental skill developed through observation, pattern recognition, and quick decision-making.

- **What It Is:** Anticipation involves predicting the opposing team's next move based on their positioning, tendencies, and body language.

- **How to Develop It:**

- **Film Analysis:** Study videos of matches to identify patterns in setters, hitters, and defensive plays. Pay attention to subtle cues like body positioning and hand placement.

- **Live Practice:** During scrimmages, challenge yourself to focus on your opponents' actions rather than reacting solely to the ball.

- **Coaching Insights:** Seek feedback from coaches on reading plays and understanding situational tactics.

- **Example:** Karch Kiraly, a volleyball legend, was known for his exceptional ability to read the game. His skill in anticipating opponents' moves allowed him to outmaneuver even the toughest teams.

2. The Zone: Harnessing Flow State in Volleyball

The "zone," also known as the flow state, is the mental sweet spot where everything clicks. Players in this state describe a feeling of being completely immersed, with time slowing down and every movement feeling effortless.

- **What It Is:** A psychological state of intense focus and peak performance.

* **How to Achieve It:**

* **Mindfulness Practices:** Develop focus by practicing mindfulness exercises, such as deep breathing and meditation, before games.

* **Pre-Game Routines:** Establish rituals that signal your brain to prepare for performance, like listening to specific music or repeating affirmations.

* **Visualization:** Mentally rehearse successful plays, imagining the sounds, sights, and emotions of executing them perfectly.

* **Why It Matters:** Being in the zone reduces anxiety, enhances decision-making, and boosts confidence during critical moments.

3. Silent Leadership: Leading Without the Captain's Band

Not every player wears the captain's band, but every player has the potential to lead. Silent leadership is about influencing the team through actions, attitude, and non-verbal communication.

* **What It Is:** Leadership that focuses on setting an example and fostering trust without needing an official title.

* **How to Develop It:**

* **Lead by Example:** Hustle on every play, stay positive after mistakes, and encourage teammates consistently.

* **Body Language:** Maintain open, confident posture and make eye contact to inspire trust and collaboration.

* **Support Others:** Be the first to offer a high-five or constructive feedback after a tough point.

* **Example:** Misty May-Treanor often exemplified silent leadership by remaining composed and steady under pressure, lifting her team with her calm demeanor and relentless work ethic.

4. Energy Management: Playing Smart, Not Just Hard

Volleyball demands explosive movements, quick reactions, and sustained focus. Managing your physical and mental energy effectively ensures you can perform at your best when it matters most.

* **What It Is:** Strategically conserving and deploying energy throughout a match or season.

* **How to Practice It:**

* **Pacing During Matches:** Learn when to play conservatively and when to push for aggressive plays.

* **Timeout Recovery:** Use timeouts to mentally reset and physically recover with hydration and controlled breathing.

* **Tournament Prep:** Plan rest and recovery during tournaments to avoid burnout in later rounds.

- **Why It Matters:** Proper energy management prevents fatigue-induced mistakes and helps you peak during critical moments, such as match points.

5. The Unseen Game: Managing Emotions on the Court

Emotions run high in volleyball, a game full of momentum swings and intense rallies. Learning to manage emotions is crucial for maintaining focus and resilience.

- **What It Is:** The ability to stay composed and perform under emotional stress.

- **How to Practice It:**

- **Recovering from Mistakes:** Use a mental reset technique, like taking a deep breath or repeating a mantra, to move past errors quickly.

- **Staying Positive:** Focus on what you can control rather than dwelling on what went wrong.

- **Channeling Passion:** Use your energy to fuel determination instead of frustration.

- **Example:** Elaina Oden, a two-time Olympian, faced criticism for her physique but used it as motivation, proving her doubters wrong with sheer grit and focus.

6. Personal Rituals: Finding Your Mental Anchor

Many elite athletes rely on personal rituals to feel grounded and confident before games. These rituals are not superstitions but intentional practices that help players center themselves.

- **What It Is:** A consistent routine or behavior that prepares you mentally and emotionally for performance.

- **How to Create One:**

- **Find What Works:** Experiment with different pre-game activities, like journaling, stretching, or visualization.

- **Make It Meaningful:** Choose rituals that reinforce positive emotions and confidence.

- **Stay Flexible:** Adapt rituals as needed while keeping their core purpose intact.

- **Example:** Kerri Walsh Jennings often credited her pre-match rituals, including affirmations and visualization, with helping her maintain focus and confidence during high-stakes matches.

7. Volleyball Vision: Developing Peripheral Awareness

While physical agility is essential, developing spatial and peripheral awareness allows players to see the bigger picture on the court and make smarter decisions.

- **What It Is:** The ability to track the ball, anticipate opponents' movements, and maintain awareness of teammates' positions simultaneously.

* **How to Train It:**

* **Court Awareness Drills:** Practice drills that require players to monitor multiple moving elements, such as hitting a target while observing off-court movement.

* **Film Review:** Watch game footage to analyze positioning and improve situational awareness.

* **Peripheral Exercises:** Use tools like reaction balls or multi-tasking drills to enhance visual tracking and quick decision-making.

* **Why It Matters:** Improved court vision enables players to react faster, communicate effectively, and execute plays with precision.

Conclusion: Mastering the Mental Game

These seven mental secrets unlock the potential to elevate your game, whether you're a beginner or a seasoned athlete. By focusing on anticipation, flow state, silent leadership, energy management, emotional control, personal rituals, and volleyball vision, you can transform your approach to the sport and build a mindset that thrives under pressure.

The mental game is just as trainable as the physical one. Embrace these strategies, practice them consistently, and watch how they not only improve your performance on the court but also your confidence and resilience in life.

Reflection and Growth Worksheet

Use this worksheet to reflect on and apply the lessons from each chapter. Players and coaches can use these prompts individually or in team discussions to enhance learning and performance.

- Which of the seven mental secrets do you feel most confident in?

- Write down one area where you want to improve (e.g., anticipation, managing emotions, or flow state).

- Reflect on a game where you applied one of these mental secrets. How did it impact your performance?

- Create a personal action plan to develop one of the mental secrets over the next month.

Chapter 11

Harnessing the Power of Role Models

Karch Kiraly's journey from a young boy with a passion for volleyball to becoming a legendary figure in the sport is a compelling narrative of dedication, innovation, and relentless pursuit of excellence. Born Charles Frederick Kiraly on November 3, 1960, in Jackson, Michigan, he moved with his family to Santa Barbara, California, at the age of four. His father, Laszlo Kiraly, a former member of the Hungarian national volleyball team, introduced Karch to the game at a young age. By 11, Karch was competing in beach volleyball tournaments alongside his father, laying the foundation for his illustrious career.

In high school, Karch's exceptional talent became evident. With a remarkable 41-inch vertical leap, he led Santa Barbara High School to an undefeated season and a Southern California Championship in 1978, earning the title of the state's best player. His prowess on the court caught the attention of UCLA, where he played under Coach Al Scates. During his tenure, the Bruins secured three national titles, with Karch being named the NCAA's outstanding player in 1981 and 1982.

Karch's transition to the international stage was seamless. As a central figure of the U.S. National Team, he contributed to gold medal victories in the 1984 and 1988 Olympic Games. His versatility shone through when he later dominated beach volleyball, securing another gold at the 1996 Atlanta Olympics—the inaugural Olympic beach volleyball competition.

Throughout his career, Karch emphasized the importance of preparation and seizing opportunities. He once remarked, "There's nothing worse than the feeling of wishing you had another chance at a play because you weren't ready." This mindset propelled him to continually refine his skills and adapt to the evolving dynamics of the sport.

Karch's commitment to learning and innovation extended beyond his playing days. Transitioning into coaching, he led the U.S. women's national volleyball team to a gold medal at the 2020 Tokyo Olympics, exemplifying his ability to inspire and elevate others.

Karch Kiraly's story serves as a blueprint for success, illustrating that with passion, continuous learning, and unwavering dedication, one can achieve greatness and inspire future generations to aim high.

Learning from Volleyball Legends: Lessons from Karch Kiraly

Karch Kiraly's achievements extend beyond his record-breaking victories and championship titles—they offer a masterclass in perseverance and adaptability for anyone aspiring to greatness in volleyball or life. As the only athlete to win Olympic gold medals in both indoor and beach volleyball, Karch's career showcases the power of resilience, strategic thinking, and the willingness to evolve.

Perseverance in the Face of Challenges

Karch's path to becoming a volleyball legend wasn't without obstacles. Competing at the highest level required an extraordinary work ethic and the ability to overcome setbacks. During his tenure with the U.S. Men's National Team, Karch faced grueling training sessions, injuries, and the pressure of international competition. Instead of succumbing to these challenges, he used them as opportunities to grow.

"I always tell players, 'Don't fear failure—it's a great teacher,'" Karch has said. His perseverance paid off, earning him gold medals in the 1984 and 1988 Olympic Games and a reputation as one of the hardest-working players in the sport.

Adaptability: Reinventing the Game

One of Karch's most remarkable qualities is his adaptability. After dominating indoor volleyball, he transitioned to beach volleyball—a completely different game with its own set of challenges. Adjusting to smaller teams, unique strategies, and varied playing conditions, Karch didn't just compete—he excelled. He became a dominant force on the sand, culminating in his 1996 Olympic gold medal in the first-ever beach volleyball competition.

His ability to adapt didn't end with his playing career. As head coach of the U.S. Women's National Volleyball Team, Karch embraced new technologies, data-driven strategies, and modern coaching methods to help his team secure gold at the 2020 Tokyo Olympics. "Volleyball is a constantly evolving game," Karch once said. "If you're not evolving with it, you're falling behind."

Lessons for Young Athletes

Karch's career offers several lessons for young volleyball players striving to achieve their best:

- **Embrace Hard Work:** Success isn't built overnight. Karch's relentless dedication to practice, fitness, and preparation set the standard for elite performance.

- **Be Open to Change:** Whether transitioning from indoor to beach volleyball or adjusting his coaching strategies, Karch demonstrated the importance of embracing change to stay ahead.

- **Stay Resilient:** Karch's perseverance in the face of setbacks—whether injuries or intense competition—reminds athletes that challenges are opportunities to learn and grow.

- **Commit to Lifelong Learning:** From his playing days to his coaching career, Karch's willingness to learn and innovate exemplifies the value of constant improvement.

Inspiring the Next Generation

Karch's legacy isn't just about his achievements; it's about how he inspires the next generation to push their limits. His career demonstrates that greatness requires more than talent—it demands adaptability, perseverance, and an unwavering commitment to growth.

For young athletes, Karch's story serves as a reminder that the journey to success is rarely linear. Challenges will arise, but with the right mindset and work ethic, they can become stepping stones to something greater. In Karch's words: "The moment you stop learning is the moment you stop improving."

Overcoming Adversity in Sports: Karch Kiraly's Focused Journey

Karch Kiraly's career is a masterclass in overcoming adversity. From the early days of his indoor volleyball dominance to his groundbreaking success on the beach, Karch faced numerous challenges that tested his resolve. Yet, through each obstacle, he stayed focused, determined, and committed to growth, proving that adaptability and a strong mindset are key to thriving in the ever-changing world of sports.

The Challenge of Transitioning to Beach Volleyball

One of the most notable challenges Karch faced was transitioning from indoor volleyball to beach volleyball. After winning Olympic gold in 1984 and 1988 with the U.S. Men's National Team, Karch could have retired at the peak of his indoor career. Instead, he chose to reinvent himself in a new and unfamiliar arena.

Beach volleyball presented unique hurdles: smaller teams,

requiring players to master all positions; unpredictable environmental conditions like wind, heat, and sand; and an entirely different dynamic of communication and strategy. Karch wasn't just starting fresh—he was competing against seasoned beach volleyball players who had spent years perfecting their craft.

"I had to unlearn some things and relearn others," Karch recalled about the transition. "It was like going back to being a rookie." Despite his unparalleled success in indoor volleyball, Karch approached beach volleyball with humility and an eagerness to learn.

Staying Focused Amid Challenges

During this transition, Karch faced setbacks. Early losses on the sand tested his confidence and patience. However, instead of letting these setbacks define him, he analyzed each match, identifying areas for improvement. He refined his serves, adjusted his footwork for sand play, and studied his opponents relentlessly.

"Every failure is a lesson," Karch often said. "You can either let it defeat you or use it as fuel to get better."

His dedication paid off when he partnered with Kent Steffes, forming one of the most successful beach volleyball duos in history. Together, they won countless tournaments, culminating in an Olympic gold medal at the 1996 Atlanta Games, the first-ever Olympic beach volleyball competition.

The Mental Battle

Transitioning to beach volleyball wasn't just a physical challenge—it was a mental one. The smaller team dynamic meant Karch couldn't rely on specialized teammates as he did in indoor volleyball. He had to be both the blocker and the defender, requiring intense mental focus to stay sharp in every play. The conditions, too, demanded mental toughness. Competing in sweltering heat, blinding sun, and swirling wind tested his ability to remain composed under pressure.

Karch credited his ability to stay focused to meticulous preparation. He visualized matches, planned for contingencies, and maintained a disciplined training regimen. "You can't control the wind or the sun, but you can control your response to it," he said.

Lessons from Karch's Journey

Karch's ability to overcome adversity offers valuable insights for young athletes:

- **Embrace New Challenges:** Karch's willingness to step out of his comfort zone and tackle beach volleyball head-on is a reminder that growth often comes from embracing the unfamiliar.

- **Stay Resilient:** Losses and setbacks are part of any journey. By staying focused on improvement, Karch turned early struggles into eventual triumphs.

- **Adapt to New Roles:** Whether adjusting to the dynamics of a smaller team or mastering new skills, Karch's flexibility was key to his success.

- **Prepare for the Unexpected:** Karch's ability to thrive

in challenging conditions was rooted in his preparation, proving that hard work off the court translates to confidence on the court.

Inspiring Focus in the Face of Adversity

Karch Kiraly's story is more than just a tale of athletic success—it's a blueprint for overcoming adversity with focus and determination. His willingness to face challenges head-on and adapt his game to new environments serves as a powerful example for young athletes everywhere. In Karch's words: "Adversity is just another opportunity to get better."

Applying Lessons from Pro Athletes to Your Game: Learning from Karch Kiraly's Discipline

Karch Kiraly's success didn't come by chance—it was the result of a disciplined and intentional approach to training. Whether dominating indoor courts, conquering the sands of beach volleyball, or coaching at the highest level, Karch embodied a mindset of relentless preparation. Young athletes can draw invaluable lessons from his methods, applying his disciplined training regimen to their own games to unlock their full potential.

Consistency: The Foundation of Excellence

Karch believed that greatness was built through consistency.

"Success is the sum of small efforts, repeated day in and day out," he once shared. Karch never approached practice casually; every drill, every repetition, and every session had a purpose. This approach ensured that his skills weren't just reliable but also sharpened to perfection under pressure.

For young volleyball players, consistency means showing up with focus and determination, even on days when motivation feels low. Committing to regular practice, sticking to a schedule, and focusing on fundamentals are all ways to build a strong foundation, just as Karch did.

Attention to Detail: Small Changes, Big Results

Karch was known for his meticulous attention to detail. He analyzed every aspect of his game, from his footwork to his hand placement during a spike. Even as a seasoned professional, he sought feedback from coaches and teammates, knowing that the smallest adjustments could make the biggest differences.

Aspiring athletes can emulate this by paying close attention to their own performance. Ask your coach for constructive feedback, record your games or practices to identify areas for improvement, and be open to making tweaks, no matter how small. Whether it's improving your serve or perfecting your defensive stance, these details add up over time.

Setting Clear Goals: One Step at a Time

Karch's training regimen was driven by clear, actionable goals. Whether preparing for an Olympic tournament or refining his beach volleyball strategy, he always had a target in mind. "You don't just aim to be better; you define what better means," he said.

For young athletes, this means setting specific goals for both short-term and long-term development. Instead of saying, "I want to improve my serves," set a measurable goal like, "I'll land 80% of my serves in the target zone by the end of the season." Breaking your aspirations into achievable milestones keeps you motivated and focused.

Cross-Training and Adaptability

One hallmark of Karch's regimen was his emphasis on cross-training. Transitioning from indoor to beach volleyball required him to develop new skills, build different muscles, and adapt to unique playing conditions. This flexibility made him a more well-rounded and versatile athlete.

Young players can incorporate cross-training into their routines to enhance their agility, strength, and endurance. Activities like swimming, yoga, or even other sports can improve your overall fitness and reduce the risk of burnout or injury.

Mental Preparation: The Invisible Training

Karch understood that the mental game was just as important as the physical one. He used visualization techniques to prepare for matches, mentally rehearsing every play. This practice helped him stay calm and confident, even under intense pressure.

To emulate this, young athletes can spend a few minutes before practice or games visualizing their performance. Picture yourself executing a perfect pass, a flawless spike, or a strategic block. This mental preparation trains your mind to expect success, which can translate to greater confidence on the court.

Recovering Like a Pro

Karch's disciplined approach extended to recovery as well. He prioritized rest, nutrition, and injury prevention to keep his body in peak condition. "You can't perform if you're not taking care of yourself," he often emphasized.

For young athletes, this means valuing recovery just as much as training. Stretch regularly, get enough sleep, and fuel your body with nutritious foods. Recovery isn't downtime—it's an essential part of becoming a better player.

Adopting the Kiraly Mindset

Karch Kiraly's disciplined approach to training goes beyond the court—it's a mindset. It's about embracing hard work, focusing on improvement, and committing to being the best version of yourself. Whether you're aiming for a spot on your school's starting lineup or dreaming of Olympic glory, Karch's methods offer a roadmap for success.

By integrating his practices—consistency, attention to detail, goal setting, adaptability, mental preparation, and recovery—into your own routine, you can elevate your game and develop the habits of a champion. As Karch himself said: "You don't have to be great to start, but you have to start to be great."

Reflection and Growth Worksheet

Use this worksheet to reflect on and apply the lessons from each chapter. Players and coaches can use these prompts individually or in team discussions to enhance learning and performance.

- Who is your volleyball role model, and why?

- List three qualities you admire in your role model. How can you emulate these traits in your game?

- Reflect on a story from a professional athlete that inspired you. What lessons did you learn?

- Write down one specific goal inspired by your role model's journey.

Conclusion

As you turn the final pages of this book, take a moment to reflect on the stories you've encountered and the lessons they carry. From Debbie Green Vargas defying expectations to excel as one of the world's greatest setters, to Allison Aldrich rebuilding her life through volleyball after losing her leg, to Karch Kiraly's relentless pursuit of excellence across two forms of the game, these athletes' journeys teach us that success isn't handed to anyone—it's earned through perseverance, mental toughness, and a willingness to grow.

Each chapter has explored the unique challenges athletes face and the tools needed to overcome them. Whether it's recognizing your triggers for anxiety like Allison, building confidence through small wins like Elaina, or finding balance in life like Kerri, you now have a roadmap to develop not only as a volleyball player but as a person.

Mental Toughness: The Foundation of Success

Throughout this book, mental toughness has been a recurring theme. Athletes like Ibragim, who turned personal tragedy into purpose by coaching volleyball for people with disabilities, remind us that mental resilience isn't just about pushing through—it's about adapting, finding new meaning, and inspiring others. Whether you're facing a tough game, a setback, or the pressures of life, you've learned how to:

- Recognize and challenge negative thoughts.

- Build confidence through intentional practice and small victories.

- Turn adversity into opportunities for growth.

As you continue your journey, remember that mental toughness isn't innate—it's a skill that can be cultivated with effort, reflection, and the support of those around you.

The Power of Teamwork

This book also emphasized the importance of relationships—your connections with teammates, coaches, family, and even yourself. From Misty May-Treanor and Kerri Walsh Jennings' unparalleled chemistry on the sand to Gabrielle Reece's ability to balance her ambitions with the guidance of her coaches and family, these stories highlight how trust, communication, and mutual respect elevate not just individuals but entire teams.

In volleyball, as in life, you can't do it all alone. Surround yourself with people who challenge and support you, and don't hesitate to ask for help or offer it to others. Remember, the strongest teams—and the most successful individuals—are built on a foundation of collaboration and trust.

Overcoming Self-Doubt

For many of the athletes in this book, self-doubt was a constant companion. Yet they found ways to silence the inner critic and focus on their strengths. Elaina Oden turned her insecurities about her physique into a source of power, while Gabrielle Reece used open communication and clear boundaries to align her ambitions with the expectations of others.

If self-doubt creeps in, let these stories remind you that you are not alone. Everyone, even the most celebrated athletes, questions themselves at times. What sets champions apart is their ability to confront those doubts, reframe them, and move forward with renewed confidence.

Your Story Awaits

You might not be chasing Olympic gold or overcoming life-altering challenges, but your journey is just as important. The lessons in this book aren't reserved for professional athletes—they're tools for anyone striving to grow, on or off the court. Whether you're setting goals for your volleyball season, managing schoolwork alongside practice, or learning to navigate relationships with teammates and coaches, the principles of mental toughness, resilience, and teamwork apply to every facet of your life.

Remember:

- Success isn't about being perfect—it's about progress.

- Every failure is an opportunity to learn.

- The relationships you build along the way are just as important as the achievements.

A Call to Action

This book isn't just a collection of stories—it's a guide to help you craft your own. Take what you've learned here and apply it to your life. Start small: Practice daily mental exercises, reflect on your goals, and celebrate your progress. Share your journey with teammates, coaches, and family. Use the lessons of these athletes to inspire your own greatness.

And don't stop there. Keep learning, keep pushing, and keep striving to be the best version of yourself—not just as an athlete, but as a person. As Karch Kiraly said, "The moment you stop learning is the moment you stop improving."

Final Reflection

- What is the most important lesson you've learned from this book?

- Write a short letter to your future self, highlighting the progress you've made and the goals you want to achieve in volleyball.

Final Thoughts

To every young volleyball player, athlete, or dreamer who has read these pages: thank you for allowing these stories to be part of your journey. Remember that the path to greatness is rarely straight or easy, but it is always worth it. Whether you're spiking, setting, digging, or simply taking the next step, know that you carry the same potential for resilience and success as the legends who came before you.

Your story is still being written, and the court is yours. Go play.

A Heartfelt Thank You to Our Readers

T o each of you who has journeyed through this book, thank you. Thank you for your time, your curiosity, and your willingness to explore the world of volleyball through the lens of mental toughness, resilience, and teamwork. Whether you're a player, coach, parent, or someone who simply loves the game, your engagement with these stories and lessons means the world.

This book was written for you—for the young athlete striving to improve, the teammate looking to lift others up, and the dreamer who wants to turn challenges into triumphs. You are the reason these stories exist, and your journey is what makes them meaningful.

I hope the lessons shared here inspire you to embrace your unique path, tackle adversity with confidence, and grow as both a player and a person. Every serve, every dive, every spike, and every failure is a step toward something greater. You have the potential to be resilient, to be a leader, and to create a lasting impact, on and off the court.

As you move forward, I encourage you to take these lessons to heart, to practice what you've learned, and to share your progress with others. The power of sports isn't just in the competition—it's in the community, the growth, and the stories we create together.

Thank you for trusting me to be a part of your journey. Here's to your success, your resilience, and your unstoppable spirit. Keep playing, keep learning, and keep striving. The court is yours.

We'd Love Your Feedback!

T hank you for taking the time to read *Mental Toughness for Young Volleyball Players*! It's been an incredible journey bringing these stories and lessons to life, and we hope they've inspired and empowered you in your volleyball journey—or in life.

If you found value in this book, we'd be so grateful if you could leave a review on Amazon. Your feedback not only helps us grow but also helps other readers discover the book and join our community of athletes, dreamers, and doers.

Here are a few things you might consider sharing in your review:

- What was your favorite story or lesson?

- Did the book help you develop new skills or perspectives?

- Would you recommend it to others, and why?

Your thoughts mean the world to us, and they play a huge role in shaping future projects. Thank you for being part of this journey—your support makes all the difference!

Made in United States
Orlando, FL
17 December 2024

56017074R00080